Advance Praise for The Hinge...

"The key to mental toughness is knowing that it only takes one. Dr. Bell takes that fact a step further in The Hinge"

— DAN JANSEN, OLYMPIC GOLD MEDALIST

. . . .

"This book provides a different perspective on mental toughness. We have to be ready for the Hinge moments in our lives."

— JOE SKOVRON, PGA TOUR CADDY

. . . .

*"**The Hinge** makes you see 'moments' in a new light. From moments in history to the one's we face in our own lives. A truly inspirational story of mental toughness."*

— JOSH BLEILL, COMMUNITY SPOKESPERSON
FOR THE INDIANAPOLIS COLTS

. . . .

"Dr. Rob Bell reminds us that we can only control our response and our approach to what occurs - but that can make all the difference."

— NATHAN WHITAKER, CO-AUTHOR **QUIET STRENGTH**

. . . .

"Dr. Rob Bell has captured the essence of exactly what it takes to perform at a high level and enjoy what you do."

— JOHN BRUBAKER, AWARD-WINNING AUTHOR OF
THE COACH APPROACH AND **SEEDS OF SUCCESS**

. . . .

*"Dr. Bell's insight and strategies for mental toughness in **The Hinge** will open doors to success for athletes and coaches in all sports."*

JENNY MOSHAK, ATC, CSCS
AUTHOR OF *"ICE N' GO"*

. . . .

THE HINGE

ALSO BY DR. ROB BELL

Mental Toughness Training for Golf

Follow The Hinge at

 The-Hinge-The-Importance-of-Mental-Toughness

 @drrobbell
#TheHinge

THE HINGE

The Importance of Mental Toughness

Dr. Rob Bell

ISBN 978-0-9899184-8-0 (Hardback)
ISBN 978-0-9899184-0-4 (Paperback)
ISBN 978-0-9899184-9-7 (E-book)

Cover Photograph: istockphoto
Book Design: Teri Capron
Photo of Dr. Rob Bell: Portraiture Studios

Published by
DRB Press

Contents

Introduction

*"If fate had not intervened, I would
never have gone to UCLA."*
— JOHN WOODEN

. . . .

When one door closes, another opens, is a cliché that has
meaning because of The Hinge. Certain moments, events,
or persons can act as "hinges" in our lives, opening us to
experiences we might have missed, connecting who we are
with who we become. That is The Hinge. It makes all of the
difference. Will you be ready?

Each one of this book's 38 stories illustrates how one person or
event changed an outcome. These are The Hinge moments
that build mental toughness. You'll discover the five maxims of
The Hinge, gain insight into a Rusty Hinge, and even learn what
happens when the door comes off The Hinges. For every Michael
Jordan, there is an Earl Manigault—a thousand superior athletes
that don't make it. What takes place off the field becomes more
important than what occurs on the field.

The idea for the book began with John Wooden, considered
the greatest coach of all time in any sport. It's tough to argue
with a streak of 88 consecutive wins at UCLA and 10 national
championships in 12 seasons. Here was a legendary coach who
focused only on winning the next game, developing character,
and teaching. There was one Hinge moment for John Wooden.

. . . .

John Wooden, Indiana born and raised, played and won a
national championship at Purdue. He began coaching college
basketball in 1943 at Indiana State University. In 1948, he
became head coach at UCLA and the rest is history.

The Hinge...

While living in the Midwest, John Wooden was offered two coaching positions, one at UCLA and the other at The University of Minnesota. He intended to accept the head coaching position at The University of Minnesota, because his wife wanted to stay in the Midwest. He was expecting a phone call from Minnesota officials at 5:00 p.m. and another from UCLA at 6:00 p.m. on the same day.

However, unbeknownst to Coach Wooden, a snowstorm hit Minnesota and the university official could not complete the call. 5:00 p.m. passed with no call. No such issue in California. UCLA called at 6:00 p.m., but instead of declining the UCLA position like he had planned, John Wooden accepted it. Minutes later the University of Minnesota call came through. The official explained the situation and offered Wooden the job. However, Coach Wooden had already accepted the job at UCLA and did not renege on his commitment.[1]

Moving a 25-ton Door

"A door with no hinge is a wall."
— Dr. Rob Bell

. . . .

Hinge (definition): Noun–*A movable joint or mechanism… that connects linked objects.* **(v):** *A circumstance upon which other events depend.*

The Greenbrier resort in White Sulphur Springs, WV, is one of the finest resorts in America. Coined "America's Resort," it has hosted legions of presidents, dignitaries, and foreign diplomats.

The Cold War had escalated in the late 1950's, so President Eisenhower, a frequent guest at The Greenbrier, decided to build a shelter in case of foreign attack. Thus, a secret bunker was built inside the hotel. Located about four hours from Washington D.C., this underground bunker actually became a part of U.S. defense.

The bunker was built to survive an indirect bomb strike, relying on the secrecy of its location and the West Virginia mountains for protection. If needed, it would have housed the entire Congress as a fallout shelter.

The bunker possessed three massive, blast-proof doors, each weighing 25 tons. The doors were fifteen feet high, thirteen feet wide, and 20 inches thick. Despite the enormity of these doors, it only took fifty pounds of pressure to open and close them. The reason one person could operate these enormous doors was the hinge. The stronger the door the more important the hinge, and the hinges for the blast doors weighed 1.5 tons each. Without the hinge, the massive bomb doors would not have moved.

What allows a door to open or close is its hinge—a door without a hinge just doesn't work. Even a 25-ton door without a hinge would have become a wall. Doors are entryways into or away from one area to another. In our lives, The Hinge connects who we are with who we become.

It will be the people, events, or moments that make all the difference and it only takes one! All of us will experience The Hinge at various points in our lives. Although we don't know how events are going to turn out we have to be ready. Our role is to be prepared and to act. In order for The Hinge to connect, we must possess mental toughness.

Mental toughness allows The Hinge to connect. It's the skill that keeps us in the moment, to keep our head when others are losing theirs. Mental toughness involves grit, resiliency, and hardiness, traits that enable us to perform well under pressure and to cope with struggle. We all will experience times of pressure and breakthrough moments and we will also experience roadblocks, setbacks, hardships, doubt, and frustration.

We control the door—our mental toughness, and in order for The Hinge to connect, the door must be strong. We also control the handle—our decisions or actions that reflect our mental toughness.

Thanks to The Hinge, the door can swing either way, positive or negative. The experience may seem negative at first—a toxic relationship, a death, an addiction, abuse, injury, any bad event. Somehow, though, our test often becomes our testimony. Our mess becomes our message.

A positive hinge on the other hand only takes one person, moment, or event, which cements or ignites the belief in ourselves— a catch, a victory, a twist of fate, a decision, any successful outcome. It serves as proof that we are exactly where we are supposed to be.

> *"Tomorrow might not be here for you."*
> —LYNYRD SKYNYRD
> . . . .

Lynyrd Skynryd was one of the most popular bands in the 1970s. They had iconic signature hits like, *"Free Bird," "That Smell," "Tuesday's Gone,"* and *"Sweet Home Alabama"* among many others, and became known as the greatest Southern Rock band. They would eventually be inducted into the Rock and Roll Hall of Fame. Ronnie Van Zandt was the lead singer and strangely enough often prophesied that he would not live past age 30.

On October 17, 1977, Lynyrd Skynyrd released the album, *Street Survivors*. However, just three days after its release, on October 20, the band's plane crashed, killing lead singer, 29-year-old, Ronnie Van Zandt, along with other band members, including lead guitarist Steve Gains.

The Hinge...

Earlier in the summer of 1977, two members from another band wanted the same plane, the Convair CV-300. However, when the flight operations manager for that band went to book it, he decided against it, reporting that the plane and crew weren't up to standards. It was a gut feeling to reject the plane.

The two band members who wanted the exact plane that crashed were Stephen Tyler and Joe Perry of Aerosmith.[2]

The Hinge...

This band from Boston, Aerosmith, had some big hits in the 1970s, with "Sweet Emotion," "Dream On," and "Back in the Saddle." However, Aerosmith struggled during the late 1970s and early 80s with drug use. Their follow-up albums after these hits were flops and internal conflict within the band tore them apart.

In 1986, nine years after Aerosmith passed on leasing the plane that crashed with the Lynyrd Skynyrd on board, three guys from Queens, New York, were influenced by Rick Rubin to remake a song.

The hip-hop group Run-DMC teamed-up with Stephen Tyler and Joe Perry to remake the song "Walk This Way," changing the entire music landscape forever.

It was the first rap/heavy metal crossover song and it connected the entire rap world with mainstream rock. Run-DMC sparked a movement in rap that broke all cultural barriers. They became the first rap group to make the cover of Rolling Stone magazine, the first to have a multi-platinum album, the first with videos on MTV. Run-DMC changed the game; they were the first non-athletes to endorse the Adidas brand, and those shoes and the band's image became staples in suburban America.

Most every single rap/hip-hop artist points to Run-DMC as the group that made it happen. The group was also voted as the greatest hip-hop group of all-time.

The Hinge...

"Walk This Way" revitalized Aerosmith's career as well. This American rock band that had been dormant, followed up the song with a string of multi-platinum albums and hits on their way to the Rock 'n Roll Hall of Fame.

One of the maxims of The Hinge is that things happen for a reason. Without these strange twists of fate, would it all have worked out the same? It's a struggle to visualize Lynyrd Skynyrd, jamming with Run-DMC.

Life is a Mystery

*"You may never know what results
from your action. But, if you do nothing,
there will be no results."*
— GANDHI
. . . .

As a teenager, my grandmother used to give me the awesome gift of, wait for it, *Reader's Digest*...As a fifteen year-old, *Reader's Digest* really didn't fit my needs. However, it did become great bathroom material and I would read it while on the porcelain throne. Well, within *Reader's Digest*, I once read a story about the "runner's high," the physiological and psychological effect that runners would sometimes encounter during long runs. It was like "being in the zone." The *Reader's Digest* article summarized a study that looked at how the personality traits of distance runners may transfer into other areas of their lives.... Fast-forward eight years to the end of college. I had to choose a research project in my advanced Psychology class to graduate. I immediately remembered the "Runner's High" story in *Reader's Digest* and replicated the same study, with no further thought.

I knew early on that Sport Psychology would become my chosen path in life, so I applied to Temple University's graduate school, despite a less-than-brilliant undergrad record. I was a hinge candidate at best.

The in-person interview went surprisingly well and, in fact, the Temple University professor repeatedly probed at length my little research project on the "Runner's High." I was actually accepted and even received a graduate assistantship that paid for school. Turns out, my professor, Dr. Michael Sachs, was the one who coined the phrase, Runner's High...

The Hinge....

If it weren't for my grandmother supplying me with Reader's Digest subscriptions as a teenager, I would not have been accepted into Temple University's graduate program, nor met my wife, nor continued on to graduate work at the University of Tennessee, nor caddied on the PGA Tour, nor been privileged to work with so many gifted athletes. My story and this story would have been different. That was a Hinge.

The Five Maxims of
The Hinge...

Remember when you received your driver's license, graduated high school, turned 18 or 21, were married, or had your first child? Some hinges are planned events—a rite of passage, acceptance into a select group or organization, completion of set goals. These we prepare for. But the most important Hinge moments are unexpected.

The story of Lynryd Skynyrd, Aerosmith, and RUN-DMC is powerful. Lynryd Skynyrd and Aerosmith were connected by one gut decision over a plane, which turned tragic for one of the groups. Yet the connection set forth a path that changed the entire music landscape in America. This story involved all maxims of The Hinge. You decide if these events happened for a reason.

Hinge Maxims:

1) *It only takes one...*
2) *Things happen for a reason...*
3) *Trust your gut...*
4) *Tragedies are immediate...*
5) *"What-if" moments never happened...*

Maxim #1- It Only Takes One...

"That was an immaculate reception."
—Sharon Levosky[3]
. . . .

Pittsburgh was a steel city, established on the backs of thousands of workers, begat through the giant, Andrew Carnegie. Winning cures all ills, and since the city was economically successful, it suffered through years of smog and dirt. It was hell with the lid off, so dirty you'd need to change shirts halfway through the day.

Pittsburgh was perceived as a rusty old steel mill city, a blue-collar industrial center past its prime. The steel industry changed. U.S. Steel struggled in the 1960's as more steel was now imported to the U.S. rather than exported. Pittsburgh lost tens of thousands of mining and manufacturing jobs.

Bill Mazeroski's home run, which beat the Yankees in game 7 of the 1960 World Series, was an event meant to happen. Roberto Clemente's Pirates 1971 championship team was also part of the civic cement to the town. However, the best was yet to come. The city needed a boost in civic and psychological pride...

The Hinge...

On December 23, 1972, the Pittsburgh Steelers and the Oakland Raiders met in a first round play-off game. Up to this point in the Steelers' 40-year history, the team had lost, a lot.

Even though the Steelers went 11-3 that season and 50,000 people attended that game, the Steel City was blacked out from the game on T.V. due to a non-sellout.

The Raiders went ahead 7-6 with 1:13 left in the game. With 22 seconds left in the game, Terry Bradshaw was faced with a 4th and 10 at their own 25-yard line. Owner Art Rooney Sr. actually got in the elevator to head down to the field, because the game was over.

The greatest play in NFL history, and maybe all of sports, was actually a broken play, with the pass deflected simultaneously by both Jack Tatum and Frenchy Fuqua. The ball was knocked to the ground and the game was over...but rookie running back Franco Harris somehow caught the ball just before it hit the ground and ran to score. The play only took 17 seconds, but the referees deliberated its legitimacy for a full 15-minutes to determine whether the catch was legal. The greatest play in NFL history also became the most controversial.

The play became dubbed The Immaculate Reception, when fan Sharon Levosky called the moniker in to a radio station later that day, and it stuck. However, it actually took a few years for everyone to call it The Immaculate Reception.[3]

This play ended up changing Pittsburgh Steeler history. The Immaculate Reception brought with it a pride and resurgence to the city, a renewed belief in itself. It was their first playoff victory in 39 years and the town, beaten down through hard economic times, now had a hinge. Yes, Pittsburgh became the team of the decade, winning four Super Bowls, but they didn't win another playoff game until two seasons later. It hinged on one play.

The Raiders were also connected to The Immaculate Reception. Al Davis, the owner of the Raiders, became the largest conspiracy theorist in NFL history, believing every single league ruling was against the Raiders. However, they actually became the winningest team in the '70s, capturing three Super Bowls in the next ten seasons.

The Hinge....

That same day, December 23, 1972, a massive earthquake hit Nicaragua, killing 5,000 people and leaving 250,000 homeless, a tragedy larger than any sporting event. Eight days later, December 31, Pittsburgh's beloved baseball hero, Roberto Clemente, was killed in a plane crash while delivering goods to the Nicaraguan quake victims.

Now there was no way that Sharon Levosky could have known about the plane crash eight days later, just as she did not know while naming the play, that there is a historic landmark in Nicaragua called "Fortress of the Immaculate Conception."

The first assumption of The Hinge is that **it only takes one**. The entire city of Pittsburgh and its course changed on one moment. It is easy for days or people or decisions to blend together without thought or appreciation of the moment. But it only takes one.

It only takes one good play, one good game or race, one good event, or one good season to propel us forward and to turn things around. The best team does not always win, but the team that plays the best does.

Most opportunities that we capitalize on in life will settle down to one person, one event, or one moment. We don't know when this moment will present itself. We may not even recognize until years later the impact that propelled us forward.

If we dare to look further at the great dynasties in athletics, teams or individuals that have dominated, every single one has had a hinge moment or moments.

> ## "Not in a million years does he make that catch again."
> — RODNEY HARRISON

. . . .

In the 2013 AFC championship game against the Baltimore Ravens, the New England Patriots held a halftime lead of 13-7. Nothing extraordinary, except that with Bill Belichick as head coach and Tom Brady as quarterback, the Patriots were 67-0 at home. After the game, they were 67-1. It only takes one. Enough hinges put together, with enough time, and it becomes the New England Patriots.

In 2000, Bill Belichick was the head coach of The New York Jets for just one day before resigning to take the head coaching position for The New England Patriots.

. . . .

In March 2001, Drew Bledsoe, already a pro-bowl quarterback for the Patriots, re-signed a deal with the team for a then record, $103 million. During the second game of that season, Bledsoe was knocked out of the game and replaced by sixth round and 199th overall pick—Tom Brady.

The same season in 2001, the AFC playoff game took place between the Patriots and the Raiders. The game was in the snow at Foxborough Stadium and the Raiders led 13-10. Tom Brady and The Patriots had the ball with 1:52 left, when Charles Woodson sacked Tom Brady; the ball came loose and was recovered by The Raiders, which would have sealed the game..."When you see a guy sulk his head, like Tom did, you know he fumbled"—said Raider Roland Williams.

The Hinge...

The play was reviewed and the infamous, now defunct, tuck-rule was put into play and the call was reversed. NO FUMBLE! The Patriots tied the game up, and won with an Adam Vinatieri kick in overtime.

To this day, try and find someone outside of New England who doesn't think that Tom Brady fumbled the football. Positive or negative, The Hinge involves one moment, one play, or sometimes one fumble.

The Patriots became a dynasty after winning three Super Bowls in four years, quite the feat. Then in 2007, the infamous SpyGate took place, which found that the Patriots illegally videotaped other teams' practices. The details of SpyGate still remain controversial, but many people continue to clamor that this scandal was a turning point for the franchise, as well.

. . . .

In 2007, the Patriots were undefeated and ready to cap off the perfect season by beating the Giants in Super Bowl XLII. A perfect season comes up almost every year but hasn't been accomplished since the 1973 Dolphins.

It became one of the finest Super Bowls in history, with one of the most miraculous Super Bowl plays. The game was winding down when Eli Manning somehow escaped the grasp of Jarvis Green and made the throw. Rodney Harrison was the defender on David Tyree, when he made *the helmet catch*. Was there anyone else in the league better at knocking down passes? Rodney Harrison later said, "Not in a million years does he make that catch again." He also later commented how David Tyree must have been meant to make that catch.[4]

The Hinge...

One play before the helmet catch was even more significant, yet most fans outside of Boston and New York don't even remember it. Eli Manning threw an awful pass to David Tyree, intercepted by All-Pro and team interceptions leader, Asante Samuel of the Patriots. Except, this time, the ball went right through Asante Samuel's fingers.

The Hinge...

Four years later during the Super Bowl XLVI rematch, the Patriots were leading the Giants, 17-15. It was the 2nd and 11 at the Giants' 44-yard line, four minutes left in the game, and the Patriots were driving...

Tom Brady threw a pass to the most consistent receiver on the field, Wes Welker. If there is one person in the entire NFL who catches the ball, it's Wes Welker. Oddly enough, a wide-open Wes Welker dropped the pass, which would have given them a first down. Chris Collingsworth stated at the time, "[Welker] catches that pass 100 out of 100 times."[5]

The following few plays included the best of the game, a sensational 45-yard pass and catch from Eli Manning to Mario Manningham. The Giants won...

. . . .

In athletics, there are thousands of plays in a season and hundreds in a game, and it usually boils down to one play that makes the difference. Likewise, there are thousands of people or events in our lives, and within these, there is that one, which makes all the difference.

The Patriots dynasty illustrates that there were several events, moments, and people that made the difference. We may meet hundreds of people each week or year, and it is usually just that one person out of the thousands who really impacts our lives.

People are often The Hinge. One individual or group connected to another. It's why networking works so well. We have the expertise and skills, but we need to know and be in front of the right people who make a difference. The Hinge connects opportunities and people. Who helped us get our break? Who connected with us and served as our mentor, our coach, or our adviser? No one gets there alone.

How do our lives intersect and connect with others at critical moments? Twists of fate or coincidences are common expressions, but it depends on how you view events.

"You can go your own way."
— FLEETWOOD MAC
. . . .

There was an American duo band in 1973 named Buckingham Nicks, which released a commercial failure of an album. Around the same time, Mick Fleetwood was looking for a replacement to his semi-popular band.

The Hinge...

One day at the California Sound City Studio, Mick Fleetwood overheard Lindsey Buckingham playing guitar. Mick Fleetwood loved the sound and asked him to join the band, but only after Buckingham agreed that his partner, Stevie Nicks, join as well. On New Year's Eve, 1974, the newest band of Fleetwood Mac took form...Fleetwood Mac would soon produce one of the greatest albums and top-10 bestsellers of all-time—Rumours...[6]

The Hinge is difficult to quantify, but it happens. In order for the connection to occur, we must act. The stories and examples in this book was a result of action, someone who took a risk. It can sometimes be easily seen, or it may even take years to see the impact. However, once a Hinge is connected, it has the potential to get stronger.

Maxim #2- Things Happen for a Reason

"I remember standing on that podium... wishing our national anthem had more verses."
— DAN JANSEN

. . . .

Dan Jansen was an American champion speed skater whose events were the two sprint events, the 500 and the 1000-meter. Leading up to the 1988 Olympics, he held the world record and was the favorite to win. Unfortunately, he learned right before the 500M race that his sister had died from leukemia. He fell... He also fell during the 1000M race and did not medal during the 1988 Olympics in Calgary.

Four years later in 1992, he was again the world record holder in the 500M race and the favorite to win Gold in both the 500- and the 1000-meter. He stumbled and finished fourth in the 500M and twenty-sixth in the 1000M. He again did not medal during the 1992 Olympics in Albertville. This was a lot of disappointment considering the expectations and years of struggle and sacrifice.

The Hinge...

Prior to 1994, winter and summer Olympics were always held during the same year. However, the International Olympic Committee had decided to switch the order to alternating even-numbered years. So, for the first time ever, the winter and summer games were only two years apart. This change allowed Dan to train and compete one more time.[10]

However, again, Dan Jansen stumbled in the 500M, finishing eighth. It all came down to his very last Olympic race. Ten years after skating his first Olympics, Dan Jansen finally won the Gold Medal in the 1000-meter at the 1994 Olympics in Lillehammer.

The change in Olympics helped Dan Jansen win the Gold medal. We can't know if he would have won had the Olympic dates stayed the same. What we do know is that it made a difference.

Most examples in this book illustrate the belief that things happen for a reason. It means events work out as they are supposed to. It also involves faith. The story about John Wooden is evidence of this premise because things would have been different if he had taken the coaching position at Minnesota. It's also hard to argue that it didn't work out as it was supposed to for Dan Jansen.

"Things happen for a reason" is usually used as a way to cope, to justify bad events that happen. It is a very effective mechanism because it can easily explain away bad things that are out of our control.

What about the good events? Seriously, when good things happen, who wants to admit that it was something outside of our control? We want to take responsibility for the good. People may confuse these moments with *"being at the right place at the right time,"* when, in actuality, it is *"being where we are supposed to be."*

We can't predict the future; we can only get ready for the unpredictable. Some people call it fate or chance, luck, or as T.V. shows have popularized, the big break. However, fate favors the prepared, and everyone who has a Hinge moment was taking some sort of action. They were taking a risk and a chance. Those who receive a big break also know and realize the opportunity or moment, which actually causes the connection to get stronger. They become more motivated and focused as a result of knowing the role that chance or fate played.

"This is like a miracle."
— JOHN DALY

. . . .

The four Majors in golf are the pinnacles to which every player strives. Each tournament has a list of alternates, meaning if someone withdraws, their spot is given to the 1st alternate, and so on.

It depends on how many alternates actually get into the field, so many either hope or pray someone withdraws from the event. In golf, players have even waited near the first tee when the tournament begins, in case someone drops out. However, since Majors are so special, the alternate list is short.

15

In 1991 at The PGA Championship, on Monday (the tournament starts on Thursday), this player was the 9th alternate! Eight players in the field would have had to withdraw, and even less likely, the alternates in front had to pass.

The Hinge...

On the day before the tournament, this golfer was still the fourth alternate, so just in case, he drove up to Indianapolis from Memphis. Nick Price withdrew on that Wednesday evening because his wife was about to give birth. The three alternates before this golfer all declined, so without having seen the course or played it, the 9th alternate was in.

The PGA championship was at Crooked Stick, which was crucial because after four rounds of long drives that found the fairway where no one else really could, John Daly, the 25-year old rookie, won the PGA championship by three shots. He said, "This is like a miracle...It just doesn't happen that often."[11]

Things happen for a reason... Will you take advantage of your opportunity?

"Whatcha gonna do when they come for you."
— *INNER CIRCLE*
. . . .

The reggae band, *Inner Circle*, formed in 1968, had a hit in the 1970s but it wasn't until a Writers Guild strike in 1988 that this band reached stardom.

The Hinge...

The strike in Hollywood caused one set of producers to create a reality television series that needed no script or writers. One of the field producers, Paul Stojanovich, had heard the band Inner Circle and decided to use one of their songs, "Bad Boys." It became the TV series' COPS theme song and probably the most well known theme song in history. COPS also became the longest-running reality television series.[12]

Things happen for a reason.

> ### *"This is the most unusual call by a referee in the history of the sport."*
> — *JIM LAMPLEY*

. . . .

Meldrick Taylor won the Gold Medal in boxing at the 1984 Olympics. Soon after, he took his 99-4 amateur record, turned professional, won the light welterweight title, and took his undefeated record into another title fight.

In 1990, the welterweight title fight between the challenger, Meldrick Taylor, 24-0-1, and the champion, Julio Ceasar Chavez, 68-0, became the fight of year, and even the fight of the 90s. Going into the last round, Meldrick Taylor had a lead over the champion, and Chavez needed a knockout to win. With 17 seconds left, Chavez tagged Taylor and knocked him down. Meldrick Taylor got up with ten seconds left, but referee Richard Steele actually stopped the fight with just two seconds remaining.

The Hinge...

If just two (2) more seconds were allowed to tick away, the fight would have gone to the scorecards, and Meldrick Taylor would have won a split decision. Jim Lampley, announcing the fight, immediately said, "This is the most unusual call by a referee in the history of the sport."

However, although Meldrick Taylor fought the fight of his life, he suffered for it. That fight left him urinating pure blood, with a facial eye fracture and short-term memory loss. Meldrick was never the same fighter after that. Famed Sportswriter William Nack stated, "Once it's beaten out of you, it's gone forever." [13]

Chavez' status, however, was strengthened after the fight. He became the best fighter in the world, stretching his unbeaten record to 89-0-1 before losing a match.

The end result of this fight was out of either fighter's control, yet it cemented Julio Caesar Chavez' resolve. He remained undefeated for many more years, and is remembered as the greatest Mexican fighter of all time.

The fight derailed Meldrick Taylor and launched Julio Caesar Chavez. No one wants to admit that there are events and situations that are out of our control. But things do happen and we should adopt the belief that things happen for a reason. We may be uneasy because we don't know the reason *why,* but we can still believe there is one.

Maxim #3- Trust Your Gut...

"Your gut is your built-in smoke detector."
— DAVID SANDLER
. . . .

The oddest, yet strongest hinge moments are "gut" feelings. Simon Sinek (*Start with Why*) discusses how our gut feeling is not really our gut at all, but the limbic system of our brain.[7] It's why we make decisions based on emotion, not reason. The second maxim of The Hinge is all about your gut.

We have a sense that we are supposed to act....and we either do or we don't. The Hinge connects with action. It may be that one decision to take a chance, to take a risk, to get out of our comfort zone. This decision will make all of the difference.

If we do act, a connection may occur. If we don't, then we just never know. The strange thing is that we sometimes don't even know why we are doing something—we just act on a gut feeling. Or we don't.

"The thought crossed my mind to invite him over."
— DUFF MCKAGAN
. . . .

In his book, *It's So Easy: And Other Lies*, former bass guitarist of Guns N Roses, Duff McKagan, writes how, in 1994, he sat next to lead singer of Nirvana, Kurt Cobain, on a flight from LA. Both of them mired in heavy addiction, Duff knew firsthand the struggles Kurt had been experiencing and felt the need to invite Kurt to hang out.

The Hinge...

Duff writes how he hesitated, and by the time Duff decided to act, Kurt was getting into his own limousine. Duff was one of the last people to see Kurt Cobain alive.[8]

These "gut" moments happen in our lives. They are difficult to explain rationally, but they are real. Why do we sometimes act on our intuition, and other times reject it?

"Something didn't feel right."
— JERRY SLOAN

. . . .

Jerry Sloan was the original Bull, the first player drafted by the Chicago Bulls in 1966. After playing in the NBA for 11 seasons, he became a hall of fame coach staying with one team longer than anyone else in NBA history, taking the Utah Jazz to 15 consecutive trips to the post-season and twice to the NBA finals.

The Hinge...

In 1977, Jerry Sloan became the coach of his alma mater's team, The University of Evansville Purple Aces. He admitted, "Something didn't feel right" and left the second week into the season, not coaching a single game. On December 13, 1977, the Evansville team's plane, bound for a game at Middle Tennessee State, crashed and all 29 members died.[9]

These gut moments could be anything... Helping someone, making a shot or catch, attending a wedding, surviving a car accident, putting on a jacket, or even picking different seats at a concert.

"I'm so sorry I got these seats."
— DENISE PRAUL

. . . .

Denise Praul, a successful Indianapolis business owner, loves to attend concerts. She and her concert-going friend always sit as close to the stage as possible. However, when booking the front row tickets to a certain event, she "fought inside herself." She went with her "gut" feeling and booked seats in the pavilion as opposed to the front row.

The Hinge...

She even told her friend at the concert, Kathy Price, " I am so sorry I got these seats." Minutes later, a major wind shear forced the entire stage and scaffolding to collapse at the Sugarland concert, tragically killing five people and injuring many others. "It was the scariest I've ever been," relates Denise.

Duff McKagan went against his gut and hesitated; Jerry Sloan and Denise Praul listened to their guts. When did you listen and trust your gut?

In order for connection to take place, we must be in the moment, fully integrated with our intuition, taking action and following through with our intuition.

Listening to our gut is a skill, it is real, and it can make all the difference. But developing the confidence to listen involves mental toughness.

Maxim #4- Tragedies Are Immediate...

*"It may almost be said, "Before Alamein
we never had a victory. After Alamein
we never had a defeat."*
— WINSTON CHURCHILL

. . . .

For the first three years of World War II, the German army dominated.
Field Marshall Erwin Rommel, "The Desert Fox," commanded the
German ground forces in Africa, a shrewd and distinguished tactician
in desert warfare. Britain couldn't seem to keep up. Frustrated by the
lack of on-field leadership, Prime Minister Winston Churchill went
to Africa to assess what changes needed to be made. He appointed
Lieutenant-General William Gott as commander of the British Army.

The Hinge...

*Before he could take command, however, Lieutenant-General
Gott's plane was shot down. As a result, Lieutenant-General
Bernard Montgomery became the Eighth Army Commander.
The Second Battle of El Alamein immediately followed, lasting
thirteen days. Oddly, Rommel was sick and in Germany when
the battle began and it was two full days before he returned
to the field.*

*This battle became the first major win for the British and
the Allied Forces and General Montgomery's greatest battle.
It would be the turning point of the war, "the end of the
beginning." Winston Churchill acknowledged after the victory
"the part that the hand of God had taken in removing Gott at
the critical moment..."[14]*

Was Gott's plane shot down for a reason? Whatever our viewpoint
on events, it was a tragedy that had an immediate impact on
changing the course of WWII.

Tragedies become immediate hinges, and if they aren't personal,
they can propel us into a state of deep gratitude.

When the bombing occurred at the Boston Marathon, it united the
country. When the shooting occurred at Sandy Hook elementary
school, parents went home and hugged their children. When

tornadoes sacked Oklahoma, a wave of gratitude toward loved ones covered the country. These unfortunate events gave us a dose of perspective that made us grateful for what we had.

I believe that there is a God, and I know that I am not it. I am clueless and baffled why natural disasters occur, why a two-year old would develop cancer or sickle cell anemia, why a loved one develops an addiction or suffers, or how one copes with losing a child.

What I do know is that a tragedy, even though we don't welcome it, actually becomes the strongest type of hinge.

There is a difference between a tragedy and an inconvenience. We may think we have experienced a tragedy until we really do. Most setbacks are inconveniences. An inconvenience is a case of not getting what we want *at the moment we want it*. We lost. Our numbers are down. Our bottom line isn't where we want it. We are having an off year. Changes are happening and we are struggling. We begin to have doubts.

Inconveniences in life can certainly be hinges, but most assuredly, tragedies become immediate and powerful.

> *"The day the music died."*
> — DON MACLEAN
> . . . .

Bobby Vee was a sophomore at Fargo High School in North Dakota when he learned about Buddy Holly's plane crash, which also killed Richie Valens and The Big Bopper (Jiles Perry "J. P." Richardson, Jr.). It was "the day the music died," and it shattered Rock 'n' Roll. However, the tour organizers decided the show must go on. So, amidst the constant radio announcements during the school day about the plane crash, another announcement asked for local talent to show up and play to fill the night's venue.

The Hinge...

Bobby Vee and his recently formed band took the stage as fill-ins, even naming their band that night, The Shadows. Bing Bengtsson saw the guys play and was impressed enough that he became their agent. Bobby Vee eventually had 38 top-100 hits and 10 top-20 hits.[15]

Maxim #5- What-If Never Happened...

"Everyone wants to be a kicker,
except on Sundays."
— ADAM VINATIERI
. . . .

In 2002, the St. Louis Rams were 14-point favorites over the New England Patriots in Superbowl XXXVI. The Rams offense was so explosive that they were coined *the greatest show on turf* and their 14-2 record and one Superbowl victory in 1999 was proof.

With a few seconds remaining in the game, the score tied 17-17; Adam Vinatieri faced a 48-yard kick. Everyone knows what happened next as the Patriots won their first of three Superbowls in four seasons and turned Boston sports around. But there is another story.

Adam Vinatieri went undrafted as a free agent in 1996, but won the try-out with the New England Patriots that season. Since, he has become one of, if not the, best kicker of all-time. He is the first kicker to have won four Super Bowl rings and in three of these Super Bowls, he kicked the game winners.

The Hinge...

> Out of South Dakota, Vinatieri wanted to be a pilot in the United States armed forces Even though he was accepted into all of the military academies, the Air Force had actually misplaced his application. So he chose West Point.

The Hinge...

> One of the commanding officers during his first week addressed the group of men, that they were the elite, chosen for a reason, and that they could be successful no matter where they were. As a homesick 18-year old, Adam Vinatieri took the message to heart, believing in himself that he could be successful elsewhere. He left West Point after just two weeks. He returned to South Dakota State and became the all-time leading scorer.

However, he struggled with the decision. He regretted not following through, and his older brother derided him for backing out on an opportunity no one else had.

The Hinge can't explain "what-if" moments. However, would Adam Vinatieri still have been one of the greatest kickers of all-time if he stayed at West Point?

He used his decision as motivation to prove others wrong and to show that he could be successful no matter where he was. The mental toughness he displayed in the decision to leave West Point is the similar mind-set to having a game-winning or losing kick at the end of a NFL Super Bowl. You better believe because "what-if" never happened.

"I wouldn't have even tried it."
— ENOS SLAUGHTER
. . . .

In 1946, the St. Louis Cardinals, led by Stan Musial, were in the World Series against the Boston Red Sox, led by an injured Ted Williams.

Dom DiMaggio (the youngest DiMaggio) was the centerfielder for the Boston Red Sox. He was fast; he was the leadoff hitter; he led the American League in stolen bases once and triples twice. He also had a great arm, leading the AL in assists three times, with 400 putouts four times, and a season high 503 putouts in 1948.

In 1946, bottom of the eighth inning in game 7 of the World Series, Dom DiMaggio tied the game 3-3 with a double.[16]

The Hinge...

However, Dom DiMaggio pulled his hamstring heading into second base and had to be removed from the game for a pinch runner.

In the ninth inning, The Cardinals were at-bat, with Enos "Country" Slaughter on 1st base with 2 outs. The ball was hit to left-center field and the play became famously known

> *as the Mad Dash, because Slaughter scored all the way from 1st base to win the World Series. Shortstop Johnny Pesky was criticized for delaying his throw home, but the Mad Dash only occurred because Dom DiMaggio was not in the game.*
>
> *DiMaggio may not have caught the ball, but if he and his arm were still in the game, Slaughter would not have scored from 3rd base. "I wouldn't have even tried it," Slaughter later said.*

It is impossible to accurately predict events that never took place. Events did happen; things, good, or bad, did take place. For example, during the 2013 Superbowl XLVII between the Ravens and 49ers, there was blackout that occurred for 34 minutes. At the time of the blackout, the Ravens were winning in dominating fashion, 28-6. After the blackout, the 49ers went on to score 17 straight points and were as close as 31-29 before failing to convert a fourth and goal at the 5-yard line. The "what-if" question was would the 49ers have come back without the blackout?

The Hinge cannot explain what-if moments because they never happened. The Hinge is about real moments.

"That kid may have cost them the series."
— BOB COSTAS
. . . .

The 1996 baseball playoffs between the Orioles and Yankees began the series at Yankee stadium. It was Game 1 of the playoffs, and the Orioles were ahead 4-3 in the 8th inning. Tony Tarasco was at the wall to catch a Derek Jeter fly ball in right field.

Except an 11-year-old Yankee fan, Jeffrey Maier, reached over the wall, and caught the ball. Umpire Rich Garcia was actually right in front of the play and still called it a home run. The Yankees tied the game 4-4 and went on to win the game in extra innings. That was their first ALCS win and series win since 1981. "That kid may have cost them the series," Bob Costas stated during the melee that followed.[17]

The Hinge...

The Yankees also went on to win the World Series that year, besting the defending champion Atlanta Braves in major comeback fashion, down two games to none, with a Jim Lyritz game tying a homerun.

Joe Torre was in his first year managing the Yankees and would win four World Series during his tenure. Mariano Rivera would also become the greatest closer in history and Derek Jeter one of the greatest Yankees.

What if that kid hadn't caught the ball—Would the Yankees have been successful? What if Meldrick Taylor had won the fight, or if Jerry Sloan had stayed at the University of Evansville, or if Aerosmith had chartered that plane? What if Gott had assumed command in Africa? No one can explain the "what-ifs." They didn't happen. Hinges did. And they changed the outcome.

"Running down a dream."
— TOM PETTY
. . . .

Tom Petty went to Hollywood with his band from Gainesville, Florida. All he had was a list of record companies from ads in *Rolling Stone* magazine.

The Hinge...

Petty went to a phone booth to make an appointment and, on the floor of the booth was a piece of paper. It had a list of 25 record companies and their phone numbers. A meeting with Shelter Records followed and Petty and the company later signed a deal.[18]

Would the Hall of Fame band, Tom Petty and The Heartbreakers have been as successful as they were without that paper in the phone booth? We'll never know. What we do know is that the piece of paper was in the phone booth and it made all the difference.

The Hinge is real. The Hinge connects.

THE HINGE:
MENTAL TOUGHNESS

"We control the door, not The Hinge."
— DR. ROB BELL

. . . .

The stories we've studied show a common theme: It only takes one. However, most of these moments were out of the control of the people involved—a plane crash, phone call, scrap of paper in a phone booth, *Reader's Digest* article, change in Olympics scheduling. What is our role in the connection of The Hinge?

Since we often don't know when that one moment will happen, it is our responsibility to be ready for the unpredictable. We must stay in the moment.

The Door and The Handle

In this book, the door represents our mental toughness, our role, and our responsibility. The handle is the specific action that we need to take. The door and its handle prepare us to connect and to be set for that hinge moment, event, or person.

A popular cliché is that sports are 90% mental. This is simply inaccurate because sports are 90% physical. Unless it's chess or poker, we are watching or doing a physical act. However, the additional 10% is indeed mental and it is what connects the other 90%. No matter the talent level, without the 10% connecting the other 90%, the physical can't come through. Here are the skills of mental toughness.

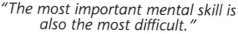

Confidence

*"The most important mental skill is
also the most difficult."*
— DR. ROB BELL

. . . .

Confidence—to believe and trust in yourself—is the most important characteristic of mental toughness. Successful athletes, teams, and successful people, possess this skill.

The Berkoff Blastoff

In the late 1980s, David Berkoff was a good backstroke swimmer at Harvard University, but not a great one. So, he devised a different game plan. He revised his dolphin kick and began kicking underwater almost the entire length of the pool, while his competitors were swimming on the surface.

The Hinge...

His move became known as the "Berkoff Blastoff," and it propelled him from mediocre to world-class. He won four medals at the Olympic Games and revolutionized the water sport.[19] After the Olympic Games in 1988, a rule was enacted to limit the distance a swimmer could actually stay under water.

Sport psychology research confirms what we already know about confidence. It's the most important mental skill. It affects all other skills, including motivation, focus, and response. David Berkoff would not have been able to commit himself to such a radical style of technique had he not believed in himself.

Actions Confirm Beliefs

"Faith is the head chemist of the mind."
— NAPOLEON HILL
. . . .

We can find evidence to support any of our beliefs...

If we believe that we are going to be successful, our actions support our belief. When we are confident, we smile more, walk tall, and feel good. We take more chances and perform in a more carefree manner, making a door instead of a wall of fear. When we are confident, we are also in the moment.

When we believe — we are more relaxed, more secure, and we can let go of mistakes easier.

When we trust — we focus on what we are supposed to do and live in the moment, as opposed to fearing the what ifs.

When we have confidence — we play and act as if we can't fail. Our actions confirm our beliefs.

"We're gonna win the game, I guarantee it."
— JOE NAMATH
. . . .

Joe Namath threw more career interceptions (220) than touchdowns (173). He completed only 50.1% of his passes and his career QB rating was 65.5. He also lost more games in his career than he won—68-71-4. Yet Namath was inducted into the Hall of Fame in 1985.[20]

There were two leagues during the late 1960s, the National Football League (NFL) and the American Football League (AFL). The winner of each conference played in the "Super Bowl." The NFL, however, was vastly superior to the AFL.

The Hinge...

In 1969, quarterback Joe Namath and his AFL team, the New York Jets, were 19-point underdogs going into Super Bowl III against the NFL team, the Baltimore Colts; 19 points!

On Thursday night before the game, at the press conference, Joe Namath stated, "We're gonna win the game, I guarantee it."[20]

He orchestrated the iconic victory, winning 16-7 and, despite not throwing a touchdown pass, was awarded the Super Bowl III MVP. The win by the Jets and the guarantee by Namath solidified his career and the NFL. The next season, the two leagues merged.

We must be confident... Our ability to believe, have confidence, and to trust is the most important mental skill we possess. Do we really understand the importance of confidence or even the source?

Pygmalion Effect

In 1968, two researchers sought to examine the effect of teachers in the classroom. All of the classroom students were given an IQ test. The teachers were told that certain students were late bloomers, and that these students' test scores would increase dramatically over the school year. Although the "late bloomers" were selected at random, the students whom the teachers believed would improve did, in fact, show the most dramatic increase in their scores.[21]

All these teachers did was act on their beliefs. They believed the students were "late bloomers," and thus answered the students' questions, encouraged them verbally and non-verbally, and spent more time with them. They probably did this with all the students. Unconsciously however, they expended a little more effort and were more personal and involved with this group. As a result, the students also started to believe in themselves.

This effect, commonly referred to as the Pygmalion Effect or the Rosenthal Effect, illustrated the power of confidence and expectations. The results of this study demonstrated that people first develop beliefs and act accordingly.

. . . .

Since we act according to our beliefs, if we are confident that we are good enough, we are. When things go poorly, we let them roll off our back because we know that we are good enough.

For instance, if we believe that weather forecasters are usually wrong, any error just reinforces our belief, and we dismiss the times they are accurate.

Placebo Effect

In 2005, Dr. Fabrizio Benedetti wanted to examine the impact of confidence on how pain medication (morphine) actually worked on athletic performance. Four teams of 10 participants competed against each other in a pain-endurance test. [22]

Once a week for two weeks before the competition, one team received three separate injections, two containing pain medication, but on the big day, that team received a saline injection, which they were told was morphine. The team that received pain medication followed by a fake injection performed significantly better than the other teams. The confidence that they were receiving morphine produced an effect in the brain that was comparable to when they actually received the morphine.

The effect of confidence is so powerful that medical research has shown a 30% change in patients solely due to the placebo effect. Across hundreds of medical studies, 30% has become the average amount of change. And, in some cases, researchers believe the placebo effect to be even greater. [23]

In essence, the individuals who receive nothing more than a fake drug or phony pill still improve based on their belief that it will work.

*"Put your faith in a bracelet, and you're
In trouble if it breaks. Put your faith in yourself,
and no one can take it away."*
— TRAVIS PASTRANA
. . . .

Every few years, a new shiny device surfaces, claiming to
help athletes perform. These products are nothing more than
modern-day snake-oil; Power Bracelets, Q-Links, Power Balance,
Q-Ray, etc. etc. etc., don't actually help athletes perform better.
However, not surprisingly, if athletes' believe these devices
work, they actually do.... The placebo effect is so powerful on
confidence that it produces the desired effect.

Since our actions support our beliefs, when people wear one
of these items, it becomes more of a why not approach, an
"it couldn't hurt" mentality, a crutch, instead of a foundation
of belief.

*" The person who can drive himself further once
the effort gets painful is the person who will win."*
— ROGER BANNISTER
. . . .

The four-minute mile was deemed physiologically impossible.
Doctors even thought that a person would die if he broke it.
However, in 1954, Roger Bannister broke the barrier with a time
of 3:59.4.[24]

The Hinge...

*Now, due to the confidence that it could be done, the
record was broken again only 40 days later, and by the
year 1957, 16 different people had broken the four-minute
mile.*

When the other top-tier runners saw and believed that the four-
minute mile could be broken, it solidified their own belief and
confidence. We often need evidence to support our beliefs. The
Hinge provides that evidence.

Do Things Work Out?

"No fear, just faith."
— MICHAEL CARD
. . . .

It is easy to have confidence when we get what we want when we want it. Nonetheless, can we still have confidence and trust when things are not going our way?

It is a self-fulfilling prophecy. What we believe during times of stress and difficulty is what really defines our actions. The bottom line is that we must believe.

Anxiety and fear cause us to doubt. Even the very top athletes, Olympic and professional athletes, have doubts. The difference is that their confidence and focus just outweigh the negatives when it means the most.

"God has given me the ability. The rest is up to me. Believe. Believe. Believe..."
— BILLY MILLS
. . . .

Billy Mills was an unheralded runner, so much so that he asked for new shoes before the 1964 Olympics but was told by U.S.A. officials, "We only have new shoes for those who can medal."

As he went to the Olympics in the 10,000 meters, he had never broken 29:00 minutes and was an entire minute slower than both the world record holder and current Olympic champion.

The 10,000 meters is a tough race full of pain and fatigue. In fact, Billy Mills had doubts, but he had managed to stay in the race. With one lap to go, he had the bronze medal sewed up.

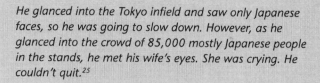

The Hinge...

He glanced into the Tokyo infield and saw only Japanese faces, so he was going to slow down. However, as he glanced into the crowd of 85,000 mostly Japanese people in the stands, he met his wife's eyes. She was crying. He couldn't quit.[25]

The greatest finish in all of sports transpired with Billy Mills historically sprinting past two others to win Gold. The color commentator, Dick Bank, ended up screaming during the end of the race, "Look at Mills, look at Mills."

He became the last American to date to win the Gold medal in the 10,000 meters. He was such an unknown that the first reporter to come up to him asked, "Who are you?"

Unfortunately, what sometimes occurs is that our own doubts, during times of stress, become stronger than our own level of confidence. We often do what Billy Mills was going to do; we slow down or even quit. The stress and pressure from having struggled causes us to abandon the fundamental belief of confidence.

We Doubt...

Confidence seems to come naturally to children, but can erode as we grow up to discover a deeply flawed world. Maybe we were hurt when someone we trusted betrayed us, or when an idea we believed in proved false. As a result, we slowly became distrustful and skeptical. Losing confidence in the world around us can cause us to lose confidence in ourselves.

Maybe we were told by a parent or Little League coach, "Stay in there, that ball won't hurt." Hmm, it sure hurt when that baseball broke my nose!

Or maybe we were given the old maxim, "Sticks and stones may break my bones but words will never hurt me!" What hurts worse and has longer effects than hateful words?

Even science can erode our confidence. We are told to "watch the ball" hit the bat or the racket, but we aren't physically capable, as physics has shown that we can see the ball only up to a certain point. The last .05 seconds of the ball can't be tracked.[26]

History can't be trusted, either. The stories of Columbus' discovering America or George Washington chopping down the cherry tree prove no more real than Santa Claus. Some of the finest quotes were even wrong. "Winning isn't everything, it's the only thing" was attributed to the great Vince Lombardi, but in actuality, Red Sanders, UCLA football coach, was the first to say it. [27]

However, our confidence suffers most when we feel betrayed by people. Even if we don't know these people personally, their deceit can impact our confidence. Lance Armstrong, cancer survivor and advocate, gave hope to thousands during his reign as king of cycling. His loyal fans, many of them suffering from cancer, staunchly defended him against repeated doping charges—until Armstrong and numerous other world-class cyclists admitted to long-term use of illegal performance enhancing drugs. Even baseball, "America's pastime," is plagued with accusations of drug use, followed by vehement denial, followed by reluctant confession.

Our foundation of confidence may have shattered when a relationship went sour. Someone hurt us, put us down, rejected us, gave bad advice, or even abused us. As a result, our own confidence was shaken and we began to distrust ourselves and anyone else, losing belief in our abilities and questioning our true beliefs. We came to believe that we weren't good enough.

The Door: Confidence

> *"It all works out in the end; if it hasn't,*
> *then it isn't the end."*
> — *TRACY MCMILLAN*
> . . . .

We have to trust that things work out. Want irrefutable truth and evidence that it does work out? It has so far...

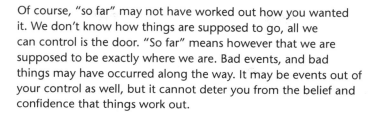

Of course, "so far" may not have worked out how you wanted it. We don't know how things are supposed to go, all we can control is the door. "So far" means however that we are supposed to be exactly where we are. Bad events, and bad things may have occurred along the way. It may be events out of your control as well, but it cannot deter you from the belief and confidence that things work out.

I have worked with countless athletes and teams that were expected to win; they were simply better than their opponent but it didn't happen. It reinforced the tough lesson that the best team does not always win; instead, it's the team that plays the best.

We act according to our beliefs and find evidence to support our beliefs. When we are confident, we find opportunities, take risks, face the fear and do it anyway. It is what great athletes do; they find a way.

Here's the balance of confidence. It begins and ends with only one core belief, and it has to be strong — It all works out!

When we are confident, we focus on giving ourselves opportunities knowing that it only takes one. Mental toughness allows The Hinge to connect, by focusing on this moment and listening to our intuition. However, when we struggle, are we still connected to the belief that it works out how it's supposed to, or that it only takes one, or are we stuck upset about our situation? Do we begin to act against our "gut?"

It's all about our confidence: We must trust that it works out. If so, then our actions support our core beliefs. We take action on connecting and creating opportunities.

" I received a letter, stating I was released."
— KEN DILGER

Ken Dilger spent his first seven seasons in the NFL with the Indianapolis Colts before making the Pro Bowl in 2001. Oddly enough, it was one of the few years Peyton Manning did not make it. However, right before the Pro Bowl, Dilger received a letter from the Colts stating that he was released. Not a phone call or a meeting, but a letter right after his most productive season.[28]

The Hinge...

Instead of just enjoying his best season ever and his first Pro Bowl, Dilger was without a job. However, Jon Gruden was at the pro-bowl and was the new head coach of Tampa Bay. He knew Dilger could contribute, so he signed him to the Buccaneers. The next season, in 2002, Ken Dilger and the Tampa Bay Buccaneers won the Super Bowl. When we are confident, we give ourselves opportunities.

Confidence is Just a Feeling

> *"Body language doesn't talk, it screams."*
> — DR. ROB BELL

Confidence is just a feeling. Our "gut" is just a feeling.

When we are confident, it shows. We feel energized, powerful, focused, motivated, and at peace. More importantly, when our belief is strong, we are relaxed. We *know* we are going to do well, so we trust ourselves. We don't hesitate and we also don't second-guess our decisions.

When any athlete after a clutch performance is asked, "What were you thinking about?" The answer is usually the same, "Nothing." It is basically the same reason why some of the greatest athletes are not the best teachers. They often can't explain how they do something; they just do it.

However, when we doubt, our feelings turn into thoughts. When we are not confident, we do not trust the process, and we simply begin to think. The thoughts may be negative or positive, but our awareness becomes more internal, inside of our head instead of our gut.

When we doubt, we ask questions, not based on trust, but questions all based on results, "Is this correct," "Am I going to make it?" "Will we be okay?" What's going to happen?" Since these questions are all based on results, there are no answers. We start to doubt and we don't like those thoughts, so we cope in unhealthy ways. What we need to do is trust more.

Dr. Brené Brown's research and book, *Daring Greatly*, examined the concept of vulnerability.[29] Not a topic anyone really wants to discuss, especially any athlete or successful individual. Her research arrived at one major conclusion between people who had a sense of love and belonging and those who do not. There was only one variable. The people who had a strong sense of love and belonging BELIEVED they were worthy of love and belonging.

We have to believe that we are enough. We have to believe that we are worthy. We have to believe that we are righteous. Only when we operate from that place of worthiness are we confident.

The Handle: Follow your intuition

Act according to your gut, not your head. You will have a goal and something you want to accomplish, but along the way, you'll feel a tug. You may even feel it daily. The more you're connected with others and in the moment, the more often you'll feel it.

Act according to your intuition, trust your intuition, and trust your gut. You'll know when you will feel compelled to do something, talk to someone, or pursue a dream or goal. Your role is to act. If you think your way out of acting, you are back inside your head—not trusting your gut.

In sports, acting according to your gut means simply letting it happen. You've studied your game, your moves, and practiced your strategy. Don't think, just act. Hesitation causes the missed shot or the missed opportunity.

*"For whatever reason, I happened
to be standing there."*
— LORENZO CHARLES

. . . .

N.C. State won the 1983 basketball National Championship
54-52 over heavily favored Houston. After breaking the huddle
with time for one more set play, a back-up forward Mike Warren
oddly told Lorenzo Charles "Lo, you have to go up and dunk so
we can win this game." Lorenzo Charles kind of brushed him off,
like that would ever happen.

The Hinge...

*With seconds remaining, Derek Whittenberg heaved a
desperation shot from close to mid-court that came up
short, and Lorenzo Charles grabbed it in the air and
jammed it home to win the game just as time expired.
Lorenzo Charles stated, "I just reacted...it rarely happens
to end a game on a dunk...for whatever reason, I was
standing there."[30]*

The Hinge is real. The Hinge connects. Trust your gut.

Faith

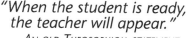

"When the student is ready,
the teacher will appear."
— AN OLD THEOSOPHICAL STATEMENT
· ·

There is no greater tragedy than losing a child, whether the child is stillborn, 2 years, or grown. The pain and suffering are extreme. Once a parent, always a parent, and burying a child is unnatural. So, what do you think happens to the marriages of parents who experience this tragedy?

Most of us have heard that the divorce rate is higher than average (about 50% in the U.S.) for parents who have lost a child. In fact, some early research suggested that the rate was around 75% for these families. However, the divorce rate for parents who have lost a child is only 12%. Couples who experience the worst kind of tragedy actually have a much lower divorce rate than the national average.[31]

The Hinge connects. The death of a child is a tragedy, which is an immediate Hinge, but it is out of our control. Is the door strong enough? If we are connected to a higher power, our belief and trust is based on that everything will work out and that things do indeed happen for a reason. This is a difficult statement to come to terms with considering the loss of a child. It is certainly not how the parents would have written this script. So, why is the divorce rate so much lower than the national average after dealing with the worst type of tragedy?

Parents that lost a child experienced a complete lack of power and control. Was their faith in a power greater than themselves the way they found strength to stay together? The groups that exist to help families cope are all about connection with others who experienced a similar tragedy. The people become The Hinge for others.

Faith rests upon our ability to trust that our needs will be met. Trust is the most difficult mental skill, and it's also the most important. So, when we struggle in our own lives, do we become fearful, anxious, angry, or isolate ourselves from others? When we become stressed, we no longer connect with others. Often our natural response is to try harder, when we really need to just trust more and connect.

Although the purpose of this book is not to tell you what to believe in regards to your faith, it is a powerful hinge, the belief, confidence, and trust, that there is a power greater than us. In order for the door to be strong, we must develop a foundation of belief.

We are only as sick as our secrets

"The reason we struggle with insecurity is because we compare our behind-the-scenes with everyone else's highlight reel."
— STEVE FURTICK
. . . .

In the movie, *Bruce Almighty*, actor Jim Carrey plays the role of God. In one scene, he can't bear hearing all the prayers in his head, so he just grants all of the requests. Hundreds of people win the lottery, people grow four inches taller, and the Buffalo Sabres win the championship. In the resulting chaos, the lottery is reduced to a few dollars for each of the winners, and a riot breaks out. Since when did we know what is best for us?

Tragedy is an immediate Hinge. However, what we do to ourselves can be just as devastating. We will make mistakes. We'll make poor decisions. And on top of that, every one of us has character defects and weaknesses. Mental Toughness means being able to share these weaknesses.

The prettiest women can feel they are ugly. Successful doctors and CEOs can commit suicide. Addiction can topple elite professionals. Olympians can battle depression.

How do these things happen?

Evil is real. Sometimes it comes from our own desires, sometimes from our insecurity, sometimes from our lack of connection. We convince ourselves that we are not good enough so we isolate.

Over time, our character flaws surface, but if we isolate, The Hinge can't connect. We make a mistake, a bad decision, and say to ourselves, "I'll never do that again." But most of us will repeat the mistake. We can't allow the bad choices to isolate us, to mire us in a swamp of self-loathing. We all need connection and most of us find that we also need God.

The Door: Spirituality

> *"God does not call the equipped,
> he equips the called."*
> — ANONYMOUS
> . . . .

In the movie Forrest Gump, Lieutenant Dan is in his apartment room after losing his legs, talking with Forrest: the guys down at the VA are always talking, "Jesus this, and Jesus that, have I found Jesus yet?" He adds, a priest told me, "I can walk with him in the kingdom of heaven." He also asks Forrest, "Has he found Jesus?" and Forrest replies, " I didn't know I was supposed to be looking for him, sir."[32]

One of the smartest mathematicians of all time, Pascal, developed a philosophical debate solely on the issue and existence of God. Coined *Pascal's Wager*, it was based on what one has to gain if God *does* exist and what one has to lose if God does *not* exist. The rational thought was to believe, because more was to be gained than lost.[33]

Like Lieutenant Dan, *believe, so you can get to heaven*. The reason to believe and have faith was the promise of an afterlife. So, why not just live your lives based on how you perform and just profess your faith on your dying bed and go to heaven? At the same time, hoping, that you don't die in a car accident.

At some point, the *church* became a museum for the good rather than a hospital for the broken. The church would praise the Lord if a drunk came into church one week, but cast him out if he came in drunk the next week. It seemed sort of a hypocrisy, in fact, most criticisms of faith have very little to do with faith at all, they have to do with religion, the church, or people…

Faith and spirituality can be turned into religion. Many fear that if we mess up, then we will lose the salvation. What we really lose is the confidence, the peace, and the rest. We must know that God loves us and that we don't have to do it on our own. We need to connect, we need to develop the relationship, and take care of the door.

But it's awfully hard to trust, isn't it? For many of us, the door gets stuck there. For some, we believe, but we just don't trust. We lose the peace by not having complete trust. We try harder to do it correctly, to give enough, or to not mess up. We even try to do more good deeds, so it makes up for our own insecurities. Our performance means we are connected to ourselves not faith.

The Handle: Faith

"Lord I believe, help my unbelief."
— MARK 9:24
. . . .

I sign my books with this verse because it is often my own prayer. Is it yours as well? In this story, a father has brought his mute son for Jesus to heal. Jesus tells the man, "Everything is possible to those who believe," and the father drops to his knees, crying, "Lord I believe, help my unbelief!"

Can we trust God to take care of all of our needs? What happens is the voice of doubt states, "don't trust God on this one", "you take the reins, muscle up, and do it yourself." The reason this section is in the book is because confidence, trust, and belief are the most important components of mental toughness. Can you trust that The Hinge will connect who you are with who you become?

Faith is not about trying harder, it is about trusting more. Trust allows us to connect.

Motivation

. . . .

A Blade of Grass

In 1998, at the US Women's Open, two 20-year old golfers were contending for the championship, Jenny Chuasiriporn, a Duke University student of Thai heritage, and rookie Se Ri Pak of South Korea.

The women were tied at the end of regulation and played the next day in the customary US Open 18-hole playoff. They battled the next day as well, going back and forth until the last hole.

On the 18th hole, Se Ri Pak pulled her tee shot into the water hazard, but the ball was held up by a blade of grass, which stopped it from rolling into the water. Pak took her shoes off, stood knee-deep in the water, hit the shot, saved par, and won the championship 2 holes later.[34]

The Hinge...

This shot became an iconic image, and South Korean television replayed it every morning. Pak's dedication and resolve drove her country to become serious about her sport, changing the entire landscape of professional golf. In 1998, there were three Korean golfers on the LPGA tour. Currently, there are more than 40, with four in the top 10. This upsurge comes from a country about the size of Indiana, with .7% of the world's population.

The Hinge...

Jenny Chuasiriporn finished 2nd, and then struggled with the new expectations. She played unsuccessfully for a few years on various tours and events, and gave up the game in 2001, to return to college. Now a registered nurse, she stands by her choices: "Sometimes I do wonder where my life would be now if I had won that Open. But I actually think I would be right where I am. It just might have taken me longer to get here."[35]

In balance, internal and external motivations direct the intensity of our efforts. Internal motivation includes the will to improve, to accomplish a goal. This type of motivation is longer lasting and becomes self-sustaining. External motivation propels us, too— the coach encouraging, an inspiring quote, a financial incentive. However, the strongest external motivation stems from the environment we are in—our culture.

The Culture of Environment

Kenyan runners dominate the world in competitive distance running. Many run barefoot, but they'll tell you their personal best time right along with their name. With almost half of the entire population in poverty, if someone in a nearby village wins a small half-marathon and a check for $2,500 that is four times the yearly median income. In Kenya, the will to escape is channeled into running. The motivation to "make it" is a direct result from the environment.[36]

The Olympic and world champions of the sport in Kenya train along side those merely trying to break through. These runners, regardless of skill, motivate one another to keep going, recognizing with painful clarity just how fleeting success can be.

. . . .

Since 1972, Cuba has won 32 Olympic Gold medals in boxing, more than any other country, despite the country's boycott of 1980 and 1984 Games. However, the boxer's status goes only as far as the amateur ranks. Fidel Castro banned professional boxing in the 1960s.[37]

A Cuban boxer desiring to turn professional must defect, leaving everything and everybody behind including the motivational structure. It is a decision filled with torment, especially in the heavily family-oriented Cuban culture. Dyosbelis Hurtado, who defected in 1994, stated, "It was the toughest decision I've ever made because of my family. My mama, papa and seven brothers are still in Cuba. I don't know how many more years will pass before I see them."[38]

"[You] can do it, so can I"

We need models to show us how they did it, coaches to teach us how to do it, and others around us trying to do it as well.

The same motivational structure exists for Brazilian soccer, running groups, AdvoCare,® CrossFit,® masters swimming clubs, Jenny Craig,® or Alcoholics Anonymous.® These groups all rely on each other as "how-to" models and coaches.

We are connected to others. We need models in our lives to show us how things are done and others to continually raise the bar for us. It is the external motivation that connects.

Models

Which people in your life have served as models?

. . . .

In 1972, William Cohlmia was managing a group of Pizza Huts when he experienced a heart attack.

The Hinge...

On his deathbed, he endowed his protégé with $10,000 to own his own restaurant. The protégé, Sandy (Samuel E.) Beall, was a 21-year old college student who would then scrape together another $10,000 and open a restaurant called Ruby Tuesday Inc.[39]

In the fall of 2001, I began graduate school in Sport Psychology at Temple University in Philadelphia. Now, I never enjoyed running, but I was beginning a new chapter in my life and needed more discipline so I began running… The Philadelphia Marathon takes place each November. The end of the race was just down the street from where I lived in the Museum District (where the movie character Rocky ran up the stairs). I saw the finish of the race. The Kenyans, the professionals, finished in 2:15 minutes and I thought, no way could I ever run that fast. So, after I went for a run, I saw the 5:00 hour finishers labor and truck through the finish line and immediately thought to myself, "Wait. If these folks can do it, I can do it." That same week, I read about PGA tour pro and The British Open champion, Justin Leonard, finishing a marathon in just over 4:00 hrs and it confirmed to me, 'I can do that.'" I finished my first Philly Marathon in 3:32 minutes in 2002.

The two models that provided just enough fodder for me to believe that *"You can do it, so I can do it,"* were strangers, people who merely did it. These were not coaches or mentors, but in this instance, they were The Hinge.

A Man Named Sal.

In 1966, Richard Carmona was 16 years-old, a Puerto Rican gang member living in Harlem, and a recent high school dropout. One day, outside of a candy store, he struck up a conversation with a man named Sal on a street corner. Sal was wearing a green beret. Richard Carmona visited the U.S. Army recruiting office.

The Hinge…

Forty years later, Vice Admiral Richard Carmona became Surgeon General of the United States.[40]

What possessed Richard Carmona to reach out to a stranger or the transformative impact of one golf shot for Se Ri Pak and Korean Golf demonstrates the power of a model. We may not know the impact until years later, but they make all the difference.

Coaches

"Relationships get deeper or they die."
— ANONYMOUS
. . . .

During the 2008 women's National Championship basketball game between Tennessee and Stanford, the Lady Vols' veteran head athletic trainer Jenny Moshak sat where she had sat for 21 years, on the end of the bench. She cheered as Candace Parker scored 17 points, pulled in 9 rebounds, and captured the MVP award as well as her third All-American honors. A few weeks earlier, during the regional final game against Texas A&M, Parker had dislocated her shoulder, an injury severe enough to bench her for several games. But the Final Four was coming up.

The Final Four is hectic enough, especially for the number #1 player in the country (media commitments, award ceremonies, practice, family). When you add physical injury to the psychological stressors, the situation becomes even harder to manage. So Moshak stepped up her care, supporting the injured athlete emotionally and psychologically in between rehab treatments, lending a shoulder if you will.[41]

Athletes cope with problems in their lives through sport. If they become injured, they lose this outlet, magnifying the inconveniences and petty difficulties. A respected mentor, as Jenny Moshak showed Candace Parker through their years together, she provided The Hinge Candace needed to return and play in the Championship game.

. . . .

Coaches provide the instruction, direction, and discipline. A good coach is a teacher, connecting what we possess to what we need. Everyone is a coach, or can be.

Relationships get deeper or they die. The stronger the relationship, the stronger the connection. Since the most important component of mental toughness is confidence, do we trust our coaches? Do we seek out models? Do we connect?

The Door: All-In

> *"It was like a dream, I wanted to turn*
> *to somebody and say, 'Do something.'"*
> — DAN O'BRIEN

. . . .

In 1992, Reebok launched a national campaign titled, "Dan or Dave?" Dan O'Brien and Dave Johnson were expected to vie for the gold medal in the decathlon at the Barcelona Olympics. Which one, Reebok asked, would prove to be the greatest athlete in the world?

In most events, only the top two finishers will represent the USA at the Olympics. You have to perform when it matters most— what came before or might come after doesn't matter. Do well when it matters, and you're part of the team. End of story.

The Hinge...

Dan O'Brien led after the first day of Olympic trials, with a record-setting pace. However, during the eighth event, the pole vault, O'Brien stunningly failed in three attempts, scoring zero points and drifting to last place. Referring to his poor performance, he said, "It was like a dream, I wanted to turn to somebody and say, 'Do something.'" Later in the same interview with Christine Brennan, O'Brien stated, "I pity anyone who goes up against me in the next four years." That confidence, apparently unfounded in 1992, netted him the Gold four years later in Atlanta.[42]

You're either all in or you're in the way because if you are following your passion, it will be tough. The test becomes the testimony if we possess the motivation to connect to The Hinge.

There are a thousand amazing athletes you'll never hear of unless you follow their sport. Swimmer Ben Hesen may be one of those athletes. The 2008 NCAA Champion in the 100-meter backstroke, he held the American record in the 50-meter backstroke as well. He had finished fifth at the Olympic Trials in 2008, so going into the 2012 trials; he had a good chance to make the Olympic team.

Ben Hesen has been a champion since high school, training in Florida with the country's best, and even rooming with Ryan Lochte. For two years, Hesen slept on a couch or on a pool table while training, completing the toughest of workouts in the morning, only to have more difficult workouts in the afternoon, all the while suspending any social activity. Being all-in means 1) you did it and 2) no one else did.

Hesen was ranked 6th in the world. There were three individuals outside of the U.S. who had a faster time than he did in 2012. But at Olympic Trials, Ben Hesen swam the 100M finals in the backstroke in 53.03, which would have actually won a silver medal at the Olympic games in 2008. But in 2012, it was a fourth place finish. He did not make the team. The difference between making the Olympic team and not was .17 seconds.[43]

The Handle: All-in Or In the Way

"And now it's all over and that's the hardest part."
— *HENRY HILL GOODFELLAS*[44]
. . . .

Can we be all-in with our coaches, with our teams, and ourselves? Do we seek out challenges or do we settle for comfortable? We must be all-in to ensure that The Hinge will connect; the door gets stuck if we're not.

Hall of Fame swimming coach Bill Sweetenham, who has coached over 40 Olympians, called being all-in the *twilight zone* of a champion. An elite swimmer needed at least 18 deliberate hours per week of pool time. It's only when we put in over 18 hours per week on a consistent basis that we can expect results and achieve success.[45] Anything less will not result in achievement.

In the movie, *The Karate Kid*, Mr. Miyagi sits down a young Daniel Larusso and tells him, "Left side of the road—safe; right side of the road—safe. You get stuck in the middle of the road—squish, just like grape."[46] Mental toughness demands being all-in. It is what allows connection to take place.

Focus

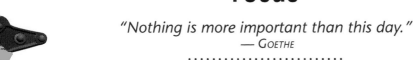

"Nothing is more important than this day."
— GOETHE

. . . .

On Januray, 24, 1995, during the Quarterfinals of the Australian Open, two heavyweights, Pete Sampras and Jim Courier, faced off.

Courier won the first two sets and Pete battled back to win the next two sets. During the fifth set, Sampras became obviously emotional, crying during a serve. Later, we learned that Tim Gullikson, Pete Sampras' coach and friend, had a brain tumor.

Jim Courier saw what was going on and offered an olive branch that turned into a weapon. He asked Pete during his serve, "You okay, Pete, we can do this tomorrow, you know?"[47]

Pete Sampras took the remark as sarcasm by Courier and used it to his advantage. He said, "It kind of woke me up to be like, 'OK, let's focus'." Pete Sampras ended up winning the match.

The Door: Hall of Famers

"I never would have imagined it."
— HOF

. . . .

Our confidence and motivation directly impact our focus. Not surprisingly, the focus of Hall of Famers is similar.

- Jerry Rice, greatest wide receiver of all-time "I never looked down the road and said, 'Hey look, one day, the Hall of Fame.'"[48]

- "Whitey" Aday, who umpired Alabama softball games for 27 years before being inducted into the Hall of Fame: "I never dreamed I'd be in the Hall of Fame."[49]

• Willie Roaf, offensive tackle in the NFL for 13 seasons: "I never dreamed I would one day be in the Hall of Fame. I was just thankful every day to play the sport I loved."[50]

• Robin Yount, shortstop and centerfielder with the Brewers for 20 years, had the most hits of any MLB'er in the 1980s: He said, "I never dreamed of being in the Hall of Fame. Standing here with all these great players was beyond any of my dreams."[51]

• Herschel Walker, Heisman trophy winner and NFL running back: "[my] biggest goal one day was to make it to Atlanta [to live]...you don't dream about being a professional football player."[52]

• Steven Dietrich, goalie in the National Lacrosse League for 18 years: "As I played my career, I never would have dreamed that this could have happened."[53]

• Barry Larkin, shortstop for the Cincinnati Reds for 18 seasons: "I thought about being good, but I never thought about the Hall of Fame."[54]

• Curtis Martin, NFL running back for 10 seasons: "The Hall of Fame was not even something that I dreamed about dreaming about. It wasn't even in my thought process."[55]

• Rusty Wallace, over 55 wins during his Nascar career, including the Winston Cup: "Growing up on the short tracks in Missouri, I would have never imagined any of this."[56]

• Thomas "Hit Man" Hearns, four world-boxing titles: "I never imagined being a Hall of Famer."[57]

• Keith Richards of the Rolling Stones: "When our first record hit...we thought, 'we've got two years.'"[58]

• Jennifer Capriati, who dropped out of tennis after winning three grand slams as a teenager: "This is one milestone I thought I'd never achieve."[59]

- Dermontti Dawson of the Pittsburgh Steelers: "You have individual goals for yourself—the Pro Bowl, to be All-Pro—but I never, ever thought of the Hall of Fame."[60]

- Pavel Bure, NHL all-star 6 times in 12 seasons: the six-time all-star stated, "Growing up I never even thought I would be able to play in the NHL, much less make it into the Hockey Hall of Fame."[61]

- Patrick Ewing, Knicks' all-time leader in points, rebounds, and blocked shots: "[I] never imagined being a part of it."[62]

- Wade Boggs, 12-time MLB all-star: "...never in a million years would I ever thought that I would be on the same stage with all these great Hall of Famers and enshrined to the National Baseball Hall of Fame."[63]

- Edwin Moses, hurdler with two Olympic Gold medals and 107 consecutive victories in the 400M hurdles: "I had no ambitions to be an Olympic track star or any kind of athlete."[64]

Hall of Famers consistently focused on this season, this day, how to prepare, how to get better.

The Handle: Focus

"So do not worry about tomorrow;
for tomorrow will care for itself."
— MARK 6:34

. . . .

We simply look too far ahead. We wonder or get anxious about how it will work out, if our goals or needs will be met. We need to return to confidence, trust, and belief.

Mental Toughness is a focus only on the task at hand. This shot, this point, this day...The more we can center only on one shot at a time, the better we will accomplish it. Can you achieve a relentless type of focus like the Hall of Famers?

Re-Focus

*"We can't predict the future, we can
only get ready for the unpredictable."*
— JOHN MCMAHON

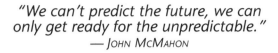

The Arkansas Razorbacks were playing Mississippi State in a 1998
football game, and the winner controlled their route to the SEC
championship game. Arkansas was leading 21-19, with less than
two minutes to play. Mississippi State had the football on the
40-yard line. It was third down and 2 and Mississippi State ran a
sweep run to the right.

During the sweep, the line official accidently became part of the
play and was knocked out by the ball carrier. The referee was
now lying face down on the field when the ball came out and
an Arkansas player was trying to get possession while also going
out-of-bounds.

Of course, Arkansas believed they had the ball, and their fans
began jumping up and down. However, the Mississippi State
home crowd was silent, believing that they got the first down,
but also watching Arkansas celebrate.

This was before the instant replay, and the closest
non-unconscious official was running toward the play from
down the field. Steve Shaw, the game's head official, was
running toward the play as well, looking at his official lying
face down, while needing to make a call.

He turned to his down-line official, Bobby Aillet, Jr., to get his
call. With desperation, he asked Bobby, "What is the call?"
Bobby looked at him, and the only thing he said was, "well it
was close..."[65]

The toughest position is stressful, demands thick skin, and
is completely thankless; it's the referee. The top officials are
invisible, because they only warrant consideration when

something bad has happened. However, the best games possess a flow, fairness, and game management. It's not like we ever see the ball bouncing around the field.

There are approximately 160-180 plays in a football game, and referees never call a perfect game. SEC officials focus on their preparation, rely on their mantra, "ready, every play" and the pre-snap routine. Every official has a different role on the field, so each person goes through a specific mental checklist. However, mistakes still happen. Thus, the referees actually have a physical re-focus cue to help them on the most important play—the next one.

Ed Hoculi, one of the most recognizable NFL referees, has a simple re-focus cue for every single play. Once the quarterback gets under center, he repeats his mantra out loud—he states, "Lock & load."[66]

"When you make a mistake of that magnitude, you kind of obsess about it."
— GUY KAWASAKI

. . . .

Guy Kawasaki is a venture capitalist and entrepreneur who helped market the Macintosh computer in 1984. In 1995, he was asked to interview to be the first CEO for a small startup company. However, due to his life circumstances and the far drive, he declined.[68]

The Hinge...

The company was Yahoo. He hypothesized that he would have made roughly about $2 billion.

He thought about it for roughly 15 years and came to a conclusion. He had made the right decision. If he were not able to accept the decision, he would not have been able to move forward.

The Door: Re-Focus

"There is no breakthrough without a breakdown."
— TONY ROBBINS

. . . .

During the 2011 Masters, Rory McIlroy held a four shot lead at the beginning of the final round. He still had the lead on the 10th hole, but yanked his drive way left into the trees, made triple bogey, shot 80, and finished 15th.

Dustin Johnson held the lead at the 2010 U.S. Open at Pebble Beach by three shots. At the second hole, he tried a flop shot, in which he barely made contact with the ball, made triple bogey, shot 82, and finished t-8th.

At the 2010 PGA Championship, Nick Watney held a three shot lead heading into the final round. He made double bogey at the first hole, shot 81, and finished t-18th.

These top players all experienced a collapse, caused by one shot. Each of these leaders followed their poor shot and hole with extended bad play. They could not recover.

These players confirmed the catastrophe model of anxiety.[68] When under extreme stress and anxiety, one bad play or shot causes a steep decline or complete drop-off in performance. The anxiety levels spike so high causing the athlete to have to manage the anxiety, rather than the task at hand.

Unfortunately under the highest of stress conditions, it only takes one poor play or bad shot for everything to deteriorate and performance to break down dramatically. These players did not choke; they collapsed. Choking involves over-thinking, becoming overly conscious to control every movement, and playing not to mess up. A collapse on the other hand, involves the inability to accurately think. They were all left thinking, "what just happened?"

. . . .

These professional athletes at the top of their game, on the biggest stage, experienced what all of us will experience at some point. They had a temporary defeat. Whatever your passion, if you are all-in, you'll experience times of pressure and stress similar to these. The key is how you re-focus.

- In game 5 of the 1956 World Series, Don Larson pitched the only perfect game in history. However, in game 2 of the same series, he pitched only 1.2 innings and lost the game 13-8. [69]

- Hall of Famer Raymond Berry, who retired as the NFL's all-time reception leader, only caught 13 passes his rookie year in the league for the Colts. [70]

- Roger Federer, greatest tennis player in history, has won seven Wimbledon titles. Yet, he lost in the first round of Wimbledon his first three years of playing. [71]

- Taylor Swift was passed over by RCA for a record contract at age 15. [72]

- Andre Agassi lost his first three Grand Slam Finals. [73]

- Jeff Immelt was hired on Thursday, September 7, 2001 as CEO of General Electric (GE), the multi-national conglomerate, following Jack Welsh, the famous icon. The following Tuesday, September 11, 2001, the rookie CEO watched on NBC, which GE owned, as two GE-financed planes crashed into the Twin Towers that GE insured. [74]

- Jim Marshall of the Minnesota Vikings recovered a fumble and ran it the wrong way to the end zone, and threw it out-of-bounds for a safety. The next drive, he sacked the Quarterback and forced a fumble which his teammate picked up and ran for a game-winning TD. [75]

- Matt Biondi was a favorite to win 7 Gold medals at the 1988 Olympic games. He lost his first two finals, going 0-2. He ended up winning 5 Gold medals at the Games. [76]

- Mike Krzyzewski, during his first three seasons at Duke University, had an equivocal record of 38-37, with an ACC in-conference record of just 13-29.[77]

- William Jennings Bryan was nominated by his party to run for U.S. President three times and lost every time. In 1925, at age 65, his brilliant defense decided the Scopes Monkey Trial.[78]

- Country singer Trace Adkins was shot by his ex-wife and survived. The bullet even went through his heart and both lungs.[79]

- Danielle Ballengee slipped and fell down a 60-foot cliff while on a training run and spent two days stranded outdoors in Utah suffering with a shattered pelvis and internal bleeding. Just 150 days after her accident, 90 of which were in a wheelchair, she finished fifth in a 60-mile adventure race that included mountain biking, running, orienteering, kayaking, and a ropes course.[80]

- Jim Abbott, who had only one hand and pitched for 10 years in the Majors, culminated with throwing a no-hitter in 1993. He threw his no-hitter against the Indians, whom he faced the outing before lasting only 4 innings and giving up 7 runs.[81]

- Lady GaGa was originally signed to Def Jam Recordings at age 19, but the company let her go after just three months.[82]

- George Washington lost his first battle.[83]

- Johnny Unitas' first pass was intercepted for a touchdown.[84]

- Napoleon Hill, author of a best seller, could not think of a name for his book. Unless he came up with one, the publisher would use the title, *Use Your Noodle to Get the Boodle*. Hill awoke at 2 a.m. on the deadline date, when the title came to him, *Think and Grow Rich*.[85]

- Roger Bannister finished fourth in the 1952 Olympics. It was this disappointing finish that drove him to break the four-minute mile.[86]

"That moment re-centered me, re-motivated me."
*— JJ W*ATT

. . . .

JJ Watt played tight end at Central Michigan University; catching only eight passes his freshman year. Realizing that Central Michigan was not the best for him, he left school and his scholarship behind. He enrolled at a community college and delivered pizzas.

The Hinge...

One night, Watt delivered a pizza to a young kid who knew him from his high school days and wanted to know why JJ Watt was delivering pizzas. JJ stated, "I had to refocus and tell myself, 'I don't want to be delivering pizzas. I want to be playing football.' That moment re-centered me, re-motivated me."[87]

JJ Watt enrolled at the University of Wisconsin, became a defensive end, and the next season was drafted 11th overall by the Houston Texans.

It's going to be hard. We are going to lose more than we are ever going to win. The key is to remember that it only takes one. If we can't let go of mistakes and re-focus, The Hinge can't connect.

We get control by giving up control.

My two favorite game shows growing up were The Price is Right and Let's Make a Deal. The Price is Right has a game called Plinko. Contestants get a number of large chips to drop, and wherever the chip lands, that's how much money they win. (Funny how even in a game where a chip is dropped, they look to their friends in the crowd to see where to drop it.)

Do we play Plinko with our lives, dropping a chip to land where it may? Life happens. But we do control dropping the chip.

Or do we view life more as the game show, *Let's Make a Deal?* The major difference between shows is that with *Let's Make a*

Deal, we have choices. It's still completely random, but now there is more perceived control. We choose whether we pick what's behind the curtain or what's in the box. We take a more active role.

Again, it's great if we make the correct choice and it works out in our favor. However, as opposed to Plinko, if we make a bad choice, suddenly life doesn't happen; we happen, we messed up. We could have won the trip to Fiji and a diamond ring, except we traded and, instead, are left with a Zonk, which is much more difficult to accept.

Trust your gut because not only will you be accurate more often, but it is easier to accept if you are wrong.

Acceptance is the key to all problems.

Tragedies are immediate hinges, because they force us to accept things we can't control. We have to accept them, but our doubts and perceived lack of control sometimes become stronger than our confidence. We lose trust. A major component of our mental toughness and confidence is how we view our events and our perceived control.

Since our actions support our beliefs, we can regret our decisions and who we are, but we must guard against resentments and self-doubt. We have to believe things work out how they are supposed to.

> *"I don't care anymore."*
> — ROWDY GAINES
> . . . .

Rowdy Gaines was the favorite in four swimming events for the 1980 Olympic games. However, the U.S.A. boycotted the games, because they were held in Moscow shortly after the U.S.S.R. invaded Afghanistan. In the 1984 Olympics, Gaines qualified for the 100-meter freestyle by finishing second at the trials.

However, for the first time in six years, Gaines had doubts. He was no longer swimming his best times and, due to his current struggles, he became depressed a month before the games started. Rowdy Gaines was not expected to medal. Even in the "ready room," before he went to swim his event in Los Angeles, he was singing Phil Collins song, *"I Don't Care Anymore."* Next to Rowdy was Mark Stockwell, an Australian, who was the favorite and had the best qualifying time.

The Hinge...

Rowdy Gaines' coach, the late Richard Quick, advised him that the race starter often pulled the trigger fast (as soon as the swimmers were on the blocks). Rowdy had the fastest start. Next to him, Mark Stockwell was not set with his hands on the blocks before the gun went off. In the most important race in his life, the starter was too fast, and Mark finished 2nd in the race. It was something Mark Stockwell struggled for years to accept. Rowdy Gaines, on the other hand, won the Gold medal in the 100M freestyle.[88]

The Hinge...

After the race, Mark Stockwell jumped in the warm-down pool alongside a female Olympic champion, and possibly the greatest American female swimmer, Tracy Caulkins. Mark commented that if he had won the Gold medal, he might not have talked to her. He certainly would not have followed Tracy to the University of Florida and would not be married to her 21 years later.[89]

How difficult was it for Mark Stockwell and Guy Kawasaki to accept what took place? Without a strong belief system and mental toughness, they may never have accepted it. There are countless numbers of athletes and business owners who simply can't recover from mistakes or being cheated. The pain is simply too difficult.

Through mental toughness, we deal with struggle and setbacks. Since we act according to our beliefs, confidence and control directly impact our ability to let go of mistakes. We have to develop a philosophy that things happen for a reason, and we have to listen to our gut.

. . . .

In the 1960s, Martin Seligman conducted experiments with two groups of dogs. Both groups received shocks, but one group of dogs was given a lever that would stop the shock when pressed. Another group of dogs was given no such lever, and thus, they had no control over the shocks they received.

Later, both groups of dogs were allowed to avoid the shocks by jumping over a small barrier; however, the second group of dogs, which had no perceived control, were now deemed "helpless." Even though they could have jumped over the barrier, they did not try to avoid the shocks. They had learned that nothing they could do would eliminate the shocks. The phrase was later coined, *learned helplessness.*[90]

On the other hand, Seligman also discovered a subgroup of dogs within the second group of dogs. These dogs did not become helpless. Despite being previously shocked, they still jumped over the barrier. In essence, these dogs discovered *learned optimism.* No matter what happened to them, they were going to fight.

. . . .

Research with people confirmed that those who were pessimistic, or helpless, held beliefs that things happened to them. More importantly, they believe that things *always* happened to them. People with little confidence or trust and no sense of control have a focus that events and that things are permanent.

Life shows us that things do happen to us, but not always, and it's rarely permanent. If it is permanent, then it is usually a tragedy and a Hinge. People with confidence hold beliefs that bad things or events are "temporary" and can be overcome.

Mark Stockwell admitted it took a long time for him to get over what took place at the 1984 Olympics, but time does heal. Looking back, things happened for a reason. Many athletes never recover from such blows.

The Handle: This too shall pass...

What I see in athletics is that one bad mistake usually leads to another and so on. How is it possible that some mistakes or even people bother us so much that we can't let them go? We made a mistake or failed and we can't recover. We don't or can't move on. We lose confidence in ourselves and lose trust in others.

The ability to re-focus is difficult. In fact, it's the second most difficult mental skill, after confidence. Our focus depends on our ability to re-focus, to let go of mistakes, to let go of resentments, self-pity, and the curse of it all, perfection. Our Hinge becomes a doorstopper if we're stuck thinking about the last play, our stats, or our performance. We get stuck if we allow mistakes to bother us so much that we become afraid to make any mistakes at all.

Mistakes happen. Ever stub your toe or bite your tongue? It hurts, but it also feels silly and we are embarrassed that it happened. There is emotion connected to the mistake, and re-focusing becomes more difficult as the negative feelings pile up. Develop your ability to move on from the last play.

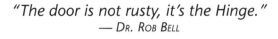

THE RUSTY HINGES

"The door is not rusty, it's the Hinge."
— Dr. Rob Bell

. . . .

The Hinge is the one moment, event, or person that makes all the difference. We've read the many instances how The Hinge is real and that we control the door and to use the handle, to take action. If we have experienced the Hinge, we know the role of our mental toughness and how being in the moment made the difference.

We can control the door and a rusty door still works. We need to focus on our mental toughness. However, ever notice that when we open or close a creaky door in our home it is due to the hinge. Examine any old door that is stuck or difficult to open and it is not the door at all, it's the hinge.

The Hinge can become rusty. If a hinge has not connected as strong as we like, we may need to fix the rusty hinges that are already connected. There may be some action or change that we still we need to make. We need to focus on the door, however after a hinge connects, we need to revisit the connection, and fix the rusty hinge.

The Rusty Hinge:
Performance

"An addict's mantra—"more."

In Orel Hershiser's book, *Between the Lines*, he tells a story about how he threw a two-hit shutout at Wrigley Stadium in cold, windy conditions. It was one of those games where he was "on," and brought his "A" game. After the game, he stated how he became overcome with dread. He honestly did not know how he did it and, in five days, he was supposed to do it again.[91]

When we perform really well, when we achieve personal bests, an odd thing happens. Our expectations increase because our best performance becomes just an indication of our true potential. Our best changes, as we get better. We are expected, internally and externally, to do it again. If we are only connected solely to our performance, this can be frightening.

Most of us are connected to performance; what we do, how well we do it, how good we look doing it, or how others see us doing it. The performance hinge is a cycle…when we perform well, we feel good, because we remind ourselves that we are good. Our performance is strong, but we are connected to ourselves. We are linked to exhaustible belief that we are our performance.

Unfortunately, our performance also has a negative cycle. When we do not perform well, we feel worthless and not good enough. Again, we are connected to our performance and ourselves.

Since The Hinge is strong when we perform well, we just return to getting better at our performance. It's fine to work harder; it's a must, actually. Except we mostly work from a place of insecurity, fear, trying to be perfect, and a feeling of never being good enough. Again, it is a powerful driver.

If we operate from a place of fear, always chasing our performance, then we believe that "we are our performance." In fact, those around us operate from this viewpoint as well: "What have you done for me lately?" or "You are only as good as your last performance."

The performance hinge is difficult, because no matter how well we do or how good we get, we will never be 100% satisfied. Even at the pinnacle, a Masters victory, a Super Bowl victory, or an Olympic Gold Medal, the effect lasts only so long. Now, no one can ever take that achievement away, but the further one gets away from the pinnacle of success, the less and less it matters. Something else must replace that feeling. Our own performance can only take us so close to full contentment and even that feeling is temporary.

Our best changes, as we get better

On T.V., after every national championship, near the end of the broadcast, the reporters will ask one question: "Can [they] repeat?" This is merely a few hours removed from the pinnacle of the season, yet the media is already getting the viewers to look ahead.

In Hank Haney's Book *The Big Miss*, he discusses how Tiger Woods actually felt more pressure after he won a major and got closer to Jack's record of 18 majors. In a *60 Minutes* special, Nick Saban admitted that he enjoyed the Alabama National Championship for about 120 minutes before he began focusing on the next season.[92]

The more successful we are, the more our expectations increase and the more others' expectations of us increase. We want that victory again so much so that we become greedy for our performance. Not a problem at all, but even the effect of winning and success now changes. The feeling of winning slowly changes over time, to one of relief and self-satisfaction.

The game changer is that our performance may not just end with our actual performance. If we are only linked to our performance, then we strive too hard to be the best. The best looking, the smartest, the funniest, the richest, etc.

It is a never-ending quest to be good enough, and once we are good enough, we find somebody better, somebody better looking, smarter, funnier, richer. We find that we are once again not good enough or we not good enough for long enough.

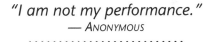

"I am not my performance."
— ANONYMOUS

Each of us is so much more than what we do. If we accept the belief and have confidence that we are not only our performance, then we can learn to accept the outcome of what happens. We still strive to improve, but the motivation is different. We operate from the belief that my sport or my job is something I do, not the full measure of who I am. This belief grants us the freedom to pursue our goals from a place of trust, rather than fear.

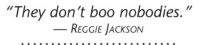

The Rusty Hinge: Arrogance

"They don't boo nobodies."
— REGGIE JACKSON

. . . .

The Hinge connects when we trust and have confidence, and most of us struggle with this. It becomes rusty, however, when confidence blusters its way to arrogance. It may look like confidence, but too much pride is a dangerous defect of character.

Arrogance, or hubris, puts the person, team, or group in a place of superiority. When we feel superior, we feel entitled, and we no longer listen to our coaches or people close to us.

Ancient civilizations to current day groups and teams have used "pride" as a slogan or rallying cry. In 1836, one hundred and eighty-two men fought to the death at a little garrison in San Antonio, Texas, called the Alamo. "Remember the Alamo" became the battle cry during the rest of the war. The movie 300, is all about pride and the battle cry, "This is Sparta!" can send chills down the spine. What separates pride from arrogance, as in these positive examples, is the connection to a cause bigger than ourselves. Pride in our cause, our team, our town, our country, our family—this pride is healthy because it has to do with something outside of ourselves. But arrogance makes us become un-coachable.

. . . .

The purpose of The Hinge is to connect, but hubris causes us to isolate ourselves, meaning fewer deeper connections. We lose the mental toughness as we slowly become complacent and believe we don't need anyone else. The Hinge becomes rusty.

"My God, they've embalmed [Nixon] before he even died."
— MAYOR DALEY
. . . .

The first televised presidential election debates took place in September 1960. These debates became so divisive that they were not televised again until 1976.

During the 1960 election season, political veteran and Vice President Richard Nixon, and a young 43-year old Massachusetts Senator, John F. Kennedy, squared-off in what came to be known as the "Great Debates."

In August of that year, Vice President Nixon had seriously injured his knee while climbing out of a car and had been hospitalized for two weeks. Twenty-four hours before the debate, Nixon had a fever of 102 degrees, was 20 pounds underweight, and was still going hard at campaigning.

The Hinge...

As Nixon entered the TV stage, he looked pale and exhausted. He wore a gray suit and refused CBS executives' recommendation that he wear makeup, instead opting for a product called "lazy shave," which only made his pale skin look worse. Even during pre-debate camera checks, CBS executives grew concerned and asked about Nixon's appearance. Despite this, Nixon insisted on going on with the debates.

John Kennedy, on the other hand, was tan from outdoor campaigning and rested for 2 days prior to the debates. He wore makeup and looked robust and healthy.

Nixon won the debates according to radio listeners; however, television viewers declared Kennedy the winner. The close-ups, candidate reactions, and camera cut-a-ways alone made the difference. Chicago Mayor Richard J. Daley reportedly said, "My God, they've embalmed [Nixon] before he even died."[93]

> It was the closest election in the 20th century. Polls revealed
> that the televised Great Debates influenced over half the
> voters and 6% stated the debates alone decided their
> choice.

Arrogance negates the role of The Hinge. If outcomes work in
our favor, then we feel that we alone did it. It just inflates our
own sense of importance and power. If outcomes work against
us, then we seek blame, punishment, and retribution. Someone
must pay, either ourselves, or someone else.

The Hinge becomes rusty when our beliefs do not align with our
actions. We may slip into negative beliefs, telling ourselves, "It
doesn't matter if I don't finish hard. This one practice or game
doesn't mean that much."

We dare not become complacent.

*"It takes more strength to stand up
to a slump, than to lift up a trophy."*
— BOBBY CLAMPETT
. . . .

Joe Theisman had a twelve-year career as an NFL Quarterback
for the Redskins. He won the 1983 Super Bowl and returned the
next season to play in the Super Bowl. However, he admitted
that he became stagnant during that 1984 season. Theisman
said he no longer cared if he hit Art Monk on the 8 or the 1
on his jersey. He even started to complain about everything.
"When we went back to the Super Bowl, my approach had
changed. I was griping about the weather, my shoes, practice
times, everything."[94]

Bobby Clampett won two California Amateurs, was a three-time
All-American at BYU, and twice won the Fred Haskins Award,
college golf's Heisman Trophy. He could hit the ball 200 yards on
his knees, left-handed. He turned pro in 1980. However, he did
not fulfill his potential as a professional. His career ended with
387 PGA tour starts, 33 top 10's, 6 second-place finishes, and
one victory. He labeled his career an "unforced error." At times,
he did not even appear to be coachable. His coach, Bobby
Doyle, once stated, "Bobby thought he knew it all. One time
he played a round with Jack Nicklaus, and he told me he didn't

watch a shot Jack hit. 'Well, that's a lack of respect.' You watch Jack Nicklaus, and you learn something."[95]

. . . .

The problem is that when we convince ourselves that this one practice or game doesn't mean anything, we may be correct, for that moment. But it does make a difference mentally.

When we deceive ourselves into believing that "it doesn't matter" or "it does not take one", we are not only actively practicing complacency, we are allowing The Hinge to become rusty. The one time we don't give it our all bleeds into the next, and the next...

The high water mark of the Confederacy.

. . . .

In 1863, the Civil War was at its peak. Up to this point in the war, the Confederate Army out performed in most battles by outmaneuvering, fighting defensively, and counterattacking. General Robert E. Lee had demonstrated genius in battle.

The Hinge...

It all changed during the Battle of Gettysburg. At Gettysburg, General Lee changed his game plan, taking the offensive against the better-equipped Union. General Lee was so confident that he believed his army could not be defeated.

General Longstreet could not dissuade Gen. Lee against what came to be known as Pickett's Charge. This plan consisted of marching the entire 12,500 soldiers approximately 1 mile across open fields, towards the center of the Union Army in a futile attempt to break through.

Lee lost over half of his soldiers and officers. When Pickett returned, Lee ordered him to gather his division for a possible counter-attack, to which Pickett replied, " I have no division." The Confederate Army never recovered psychologically from this error. This became known as the turning point of the war and the high-water mark of the Confederacy.[96]

Arrogance prevents us from connecting, because we feel [this] person, practice, event, meeting, or trip is not worth it. We don't know when that one moment or person will present itself, but pride will prevent the connection.

> *"To give anything less than our best means to sacrifice the gift."*
> — STEVE PREFONTAINE

We control the door and the handle, and our role is to keep giving ourselves opportunities. When we become complacent— we believe our best is not necessary. When we become prideful—we believe it is all up to me. When we become un-coachable—we isolate and reject help. The hinge becomes rusty when we become prideful, complacent, or un-coachable.

The Rusty Hinge:
High Expectations

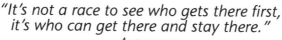

*"It's not a race to see who gets there first,
it's who can get there and stay there."*
— ANONYMOUS

....

In 1998, David Gossett was the Big-12 player of the year at Texas University, freshman of the year, and first team All-American. In 1999, he won the U.S. Amateur in dominating fashion, beating his opponent 9&8. He turned pro later that summer, after playing in The Masters and the U.S. Open. He struggled his first year on tour, playing under sponsors' exemptions, and even shot a highlight round of 59 in a qualifying school.[97]

In 2001, playing in his fifth career PGA Tour start at The John Deere Classic, David Gossett won the event! He also played strong in 2002 as well, finishing 100th on the money list and keeping his tour card.

The Hinge...

His golf began to unravel in 2003, beset by some family issues and golf swing problems. In 2004, he made only 2 cuts in 25 starts on the PGA Tour and lost his status.[97]

David Gossett's story is one of the highest of expectations. From 2008 to 2012, David Gossett played in 43 mini-tour events, and made the cut in only 13 of them. A far cry from when he had 6 top 10's in one season on the PGA Tour. The result was articles such as, What happened to David Gossett, in the 2004 issue of Sports Illustrated, followed by years of continued play on the mini-tours. He is still out there today, grinding away.

Top sports teams are in large cities, but many of the top athletes are from small towns. Nearly half of the NFL'ers and PGA tour players, and even 30% of NBA'ers come from small towns. Other factors come into play as well, but clearly being a big fish in a little pond can have a positive effect on an athlete's confidence.[98]

In essence, as youth, we develop our sense of self and our confidence from our peer group. Small towns can produce opportunities for early success, to be one of, if not the best, player. Success breeds success, and since we're confident, we want to play more. So, our confidence also affects our motivation in an upward spiral.

Small towns also identify with and take more pride in their high school athletics and "their" sports, more so than a large city. Thus, there are even more built-up expectations and recognition for their stars.

Sometimes, however, there can be a negative effect on the big fish as they enter larger waters. Most often, the big fish/ small pond effect wears off at the collegiate level. These athletes attend the most competitive DI schools and discover that their new teammates and competitors are as talented as they are. What worked before (i.e., their sheer talent) must be enhanced with changes, coaching, and work ethic. If The Hinge isn't strong, expectations causes the Hinge to become rusty.

"The best high-school player I ever saw."
— LOU HOLTZ
. . . .

Very few folks ever left Randy Moss' small town of Dupont, West Virginia, and they either worked in the coalmines or chemical factories. As a freshman in high school, Randy Moss had expectations placed upon him by everyone in the town, realizing his giftedness and potential.

Lou Holtz said, "he was the best high-school player he ever saw." His high-school coach, Dick Whitman, stated after a summer freshman practice that "he could be as good as Jerry Rice."

Randy Moss, in 1995, was in high school, while backing-up a friend in a racially motivated fight, he allegedly kicked a student and ruptured the student's spleen. He subsequently lost his scholarship to Notre Dame, spent 30 days in jail, and later had to red-shirt at Florida State. However, while at Florida State, he failed a drug test for marijuana and was released from that team as well. He transferred to Marshall University, where he excelled, and was later drafted in the late first round of the NFL draft.[99]

Randy Moss has had a great career in the NFL and will probably be a Hall of Famer, but he often had a cloud of controversy and what could have been. Except the Hinge can't explain "what-if" moments.

. . . .

Much of the development of sport stars involves *expectations*. Confidence is something within our control; however, expectations are outside of our control. Expectations from ourselves are usually a positive thing, however, when they are placed upon us from others, they can turn into pressure. So when the highest of expectations are placed upon young "can't miss" athletes, it is difficult. We need to return our belief that it only takes one...

The Rusty Hinge: "Don't"

*"Be careful what you say to yourself
because you're listening."*
— LISA HAYES

. . . .

On October 25, 1986, The Boston Red Sox were up 5-3 in the 10th inning. They were 3 outs away from their first World Series since 1918. The Mets, however, rallied for 3 straight singles. The next play was a slow roller by Mookie Wilson up the first base line. It went through Bill Buckner's legs and became known as the most costly error in all of sports.

The Hinge...

On October 9, three weeks before the costly error, Bill Buckner was giving an interview, wherein he said, "The dreams are that you're gonna have a great series and win. The nightmares are that you're gonna let the winning run score on a ground ball through your legs. Those things happen, you know. I think a lot of it is just fate."[100]

American social psychologist Daniel Wegner conducted an important research study in 1987. The researchers wanted to see how people suppressed their own thoughts. Study participants were asked to verbalize their thoughts continually for five straight minutes and to ring a bell if they thought or verbalized a "white bear." The researcher, however, gave specific instructions before the five-minute session began: " Try NOT to think of a white bear."[101]

Wegner's research showed that most individuals became preoccupied with trying not to think about a certain object. A meaningless object, such as a white bear, became lodged in the mind, and it would surface during moments of weakness. The real world application from this experiment is more pronounced, because we, as individuals, can become preoccupied with more significant thoughts other than a white bear. Worse is that the more we try to suppress it, it can create a rebound effect of pre-occupation.

Our minds are just like a pitcher in baseball. The pitcher will only remember the very *last thing said* by the coach. So, if the coach mistakenly walks off the mound saying, *"Don't walk him,"* it is stuck in the head of the pitcher. Unless he can replace that thought of *"don't,"* he will pitch trying NOT to walk him.

Our mental toughness is directly connected with our thoughts. We say what we don't want to happen, instead of telling ourselves what we do want. We notice the danger and the bad things that can happen and become pre-occupied.

Thoughts of "don't" will just pop in our mind often; "Don't miss it", "don't hit it here." We will also hear "don't" from others; "Don't drop it," or "don't listen to them." It can even become weaved into our mental fabric; "don't do that," or "don't trust them."

In early man times, noticing the danger of an animal was a survival technique. Those with heightened awareness survived, and those who didn't notice the dangers fast enough, died. It became part of our nature and disposition to locate, find, and anticipate the immediate danger. Over thousands of years, the need for this survival technique diminished somewhat, but just like our appendix, we kept it.

So, today, we still notice what we do not want to happen, the dangers of what could go wrong. Under times of stress, the preoccupation becomes most prominent; our thoughts become filled with "don't." When we isolate, these thoughts become more prominent and The Hinge becomes rusty.

In part, this same disposition is what has caused more generalized anxiety in today's culture. We are more anxious, more fearful, and more focused on what we don't want to do and what could go wrong. In fact, if you want someone to do something, tell them, "don't."

Thankfully, Wegner and colleagues (1987) found that there was relief from trying "not" to think of something. The key was to actively replace the undesirable thought with a single active interest.[101]

That's mental toughness.

OFF THE HINGES

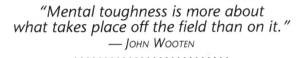

*"Mental toughness is more about
what takes place off the field than on it."*
— JOHN WOOTEN

. . . .

Usually, The Hinge gets rusty before the door comes off. Our confidence and mental toughness won't allow us to prop our door wide-open and expect it to stay that way. We will still have doubts, fear, setbacks, adversity, negative people, and stinking thinking. Our mental toughness is necessary to have confidence, focus, and re-focus. However, the door can still come off The Hinges. It only takes one…

"Kick the door off the hinge."
— NELLY

. . . .

Roy Raymond felt embarrassed the first time he walked into a department store to buy a negligee for his wife, Victoria. So, he got a $40,000 loan and borrowed another $40,000 to open a store, Victoria's Secret, specifically designed to sell lingerie. He made $500,000 in the first year alone, opened up three more stores, and even a catalog. He sold the company after five years for $2.6 million.

Off The Hinges…

Close to a three million dollar pay day was not bad, except that Victoria's Secret became the largest American lingerie retailer, grossing over $1 billion just eight years later. Roy Raymond believed in his dream, but not enough to see it all the way through to the end. He knew he made a mistake and could not overcome it. In 1993, a few failed business ventures later, Roy Raymond committed suicide by jumping off the Golden Gate Bridge.[102]

The unfortunate part is that Roy Raymond believed, but he did not trust in it enough to see what it could have become. The Hinge became rusty and he did not effectively handle the difficult defeats.

*"All for nothing, just because
I wanted to have a good time."*
— JAMES BANKS
. . . .

James Banks was Mr. Football in Indiana, 3rd ranked quarterback in the nation in 2002, and one of the "can't miss" prospects. At the very least, he was going to get an opportunity in the NFL. Everyone knows a James Banks— just think of the absolute best player you ever saw.

James Banks played football at Ben Davis High School in Indianapolis for Hall of Fame coach, Dick Dullaghan, who said, "He was the best player I ever coached," which included six state championships. A few stats from his junior and senior season alone included passing for 3,215 yards and 39 TDs and rushing for 1,665 yards and 23 TDs. He was so skilled, that he even won defensive player of the year in football his senior season, in addition to being all-state in basketball and track, running a 10.6 in the100m.

In 2001, in the regional semi-final game, James Banks was punting (he was the punter, too) and the snap flew over his head. He retrieved it at the four-yard line and what happened next made the legend grow. He actually shimmied before running all the way to the right side of the field, cutting completely back across the field not even passing the 20-yard line, then made one more move, and was gone down the field, scoring a touchdown, a 96-yd broken play TD in the biggest game of the year.

James Banks signed at The University of Tennessee (UT) and, even as a freshman, he was a difference maker. He was converted to wide receiver and led the team in receptions by his sophomore season. He still made highlight reel plays, catching a Hail-Mary pass against Florida in 2003, during the last play of the half, in a game they ended up winning. However, The Hinge came off the door for James Banks.

It was not a lack of work ethic or drive, which can sometimes plague really great athletes. What derailed James Banks was the environment he found himself in, the culture of football at UT. Members of this team accumulated 20 different incidents at The University of Tennessee during 2004, including shoplifting, assault, gun charges, motor vehicle citations, and disturbing the peace. Unfortunately, James Banks was a part of the culture.[103]

James Banks had altercations with the police, ranging from playing loud music to underage drinking, and he also had altercations with a female student and missed football meetings at UT, and then he injured his knee. When an athlete gets injured and has to rehab, he now has free time, which can be dangerous. Banks admitted to smoking marijuana during his rehab and, although he was going to sit out the first three games of the season, he failed a drug test and was dismissed from the team. James Banks transferred schools and even played a little bit in the CFL, but he never made it past limited practice squad status in the NFL.

"Well, it would have to be 'The Goat.'"
— KAREEM ABDUL-JABBAR

Kareem Abdul-Jabbar was asked at the end of his Hall of Fame career, when he had his number retired, who was the best player he ever played against. Considering he played against some pretty awesome NBA'ers, the answer should have been a good one. Except, Kareem paused and then answered, "Well, it would have to be 'The Goat.'"[104]

He was referring to Earl Manigault, a player who honed his talent on and off the streets of Harlem at the famous Rucker Park. Manigault's commitment, desire, and ability were legendary. He would practice hundreds of shots every day, even practicing with ankle weights on. At 6'2", he could pick quarters off the top of the backboard, and once won a $60 bet by reverse dunking 36 times in a row. But he didn't follow rules well. Earl often smoked marijuana, and was kicked out of high school. In college, he struggled with the coach and was released from the team. Back on the streets of Harlem, he began using heroin and ended up serving jail time. The best player Kareem Abdul-Jabbar could name never made it.

"I can't blame nobody, I have to blame myself."
— JONATHON HARGETT

. . . .

Another possible NBA Hall of Famer, Amar'e Stoudemire, was asked who was the greatest player he played against. He said, "[Jonathon] Hargett is probably, by far, the best player I've ever played with." Jonathon Hargett was from Richmond, Virginia, and was constantly compared to Allen Iverson, due to his quickness, athleticism, range, and ball skills. He was a top-10 recruit in 2001, and some NBA scouts projected he could be the first point guard to jump directly to the league. He even had his own play, called the "Hargett," which was a lob off the backboard to himself for a one-arm jam.[105]

However, even as a fifteen year-old, he was offered $20,000 to play in college, and habitually used marijuana, as well as selling $1,000 worth of cocaine a day. He started off college well, although a slight injury during his freshman season at West Virginia University (WVU) and a poor season, followed by the NCAA ruling him ineligible, caused him to miss his early NBA window and went undrafted. Although he tried to make a comeback at a Division II school, he was still ineligible, and was eventually arrested for cocaine distribution.[105]

"Where everyone waves to everybody, except you."
— DR. ROB BELL

. . . .

The Hinge came off the door for me. While I was never on the level of these freakish athletes just mentioned, I was at least okay. However, like so many talented amateur and professional athletes, partying unhinged me. I lost my senior season in high school, and the behavior carried over into college.

Five days after I turned eighteen (now a legal adult), I was arrested at a party and kicked off the high-school soccer team. I liked soccer and was good, but it was never my absolute passion. Still, getting kicked off the team removed any option of playing in college and affected my life in small-town Maryland. I was now a "bad kid," and in a small town, where everyone waves to everybody *except you*, this was painful.

I could have rebounded from this mistake, except I didn't. I lacked the mental toughness to re-focus.

The door came off The Hinge during college, when I went to play baseball in a small school in West Virginia. Late one night, I actually walked off an 80-foot cliff. The response team actually had to crane me up out of the ravine. Despite breaking my wrist, injuring my back, and ripping open my skull, I was alive.

. . . .

It was a personal tragedy for me and one that I never entirely recovered from because there was so much regret for never having played in college. Perhaps I walked off the cliff for a reason because it demanded mental toughness to use my experiences to help others. My mess became my message.

It only takes one…Drinking and drugs are the simplest way to cope with setbacks and the fastest way for the door to come off The Hinge. However, if we can learn to recognize a rusty Hinge before it comes off, we can choose to turn things around. Mental toughness allows us to see the rust forming, usually off the field. It's never too late.

The Most Important Hinge

"They are going to bury you in the ground just like everybody else and they will ask, what did he do."
— COACH HERMAN BOONE

. . . .

Chris Chelios had not been recruited by any college hockey programs out of high school, and had just been cut by his 2nd junior B hockey team in Canada. He was at a low point at a Detroit bus stop with no fare to get back to his home in San Diego. He even begged the ticket clerk to allow him to mail the money back. However, two brothers overheard his pleas and gave him the bus fare for the trip home.[106]

The Hinge...

The two guys who lent Chris the bus fare owned the farm where Lynyrd Skynyrd's plane crashed. Chris Chelios worked harder than ever that year, gaining 40 pounds of muscle on his way to the Hall of Fame.

We don't know the impact one person or one moment will have on our lives. Since The Hinge can't explain "what-if" moments, we can't know the far-reaching impact the same plane crash mentioned at the beginning of this book would have on Chris Chelios. What we do know is that it made a difference.

We also don't know when The Hinge will happen. It could be an event, a moment, or person that makes the difference. What we need to do is take care of the door and the handle, our mental toughness. We must have confidence and believe that it works out in the end. This belief allows us to be all-in, to trust and connect with others, and to keep giving ourselves opportunities. When we trust, we take action and perform with less fear of how it will work out. When we believe, we also develop the focus we need and learn to let go of mistakes that can burden us.

"Have a Purpose."
— IAN JENKINS
. . . .

- A top-15 youth goaltender in the country, Ian Jenkins, would write on his mitt, and leg pads, "H.A.P."- Have A Purpose.[107]

- Justin Cross, a collegiate golfer, wore a bracelet on his wrist that read "A1"- Audience of one.[108]

- Every season, Iowa basketball awards the player with the best spirit, enthusiasm, and intensity. An Iowan born player on rival, Iowa State, wears the number 40. Both of these traditions are due to Chris Street.[109]

- Every 3rd Friday, all-across the country, fathers and kids get together for a Dad's Day breakfast. This tradition was built because of a student-athlete, John Bissmeyer, who played linebacker in high school.[110]

- Fran Crippen, a six-time U.S. national champion in open water swimming, and a gold medal winner at the Pan American Games, had a foundation created, called FCEF- Fran Crippen Elevation Foundation. His saying was "work the dream."[111]

- Greg Oden hosts the Travis Smith Memorial Golf Classic every August. Travis Smith was a collegiate golfer and he and Oden were best friends growing up.[112]

These examples are athletes who created a lasting legacy, something bigger than themselves. They created a connection for others. Unfortunately, these athletes also died during their careers.

The most important hinge will be the connection for others. Our mental toughness is rooted in confidence, that we know that we are good enough. We understand that our performance is not only who we are; we'll struggle and make mistakes, but we also can still be the connection for others.

Coaches and educators are built to be the connection for others. We can influence in different ways, as a friend, colleague, partner, parent, or teammate.

The Hinge may even be a fellow competitor, the person that helped drive us to be better. Ali had Frazier, Nicklaus had Palmer, Magic had Bird, Coe had Ovett, Federer had Nadal, Navratilova had Evert...

The Hinge is about connection, and it's why we are here. The digital age and the web have made connection readily available and so simple that we can connect with basically anyone. However, it is the strength of these connections that really matters. Just having over 1200 friends on social media doesn't mean that we can call any of them up.

> *"Our mess, becomes our message."*
> — ROBIN ROBERTS
> . . . .

Relationships get deeper or they die. The most important Hinge is the one we are for others. The Hinge is real and it connects and it only takes one.

We don't know when we will be The Hinge for others; we may never know our impact or influence. That's why connection is so important. We must take chances and calculated risks. We must share our story and our insecurities with others. We must believe. If we listen to our gut, that tug we will feel, it will help direct our path.

The irony is that when we help others achieve their goals, it actually helps us achieve ours. When we listen to or help others, it gets us away from our own issues and problems. We become the one's that benefit most from connecting with others, but we have to give it away. We can only connect, when we take action, and give ourselves opportunities.

You are now aware...

The Hinge is real. The Hinge connects...

The Serenity Prayer

God Grant me the serenity

to accept the things I cannot change;

the courage to change the things I can;

and the wisdom to know the difference.

Living one day at a time;

Enjoying one moment at a time;

Accepting hardships as the pathway to peace;

Taking as He did, this sinful world as it is,
not as I would have it;

Trusting that he will make all things
right if I surrender to His Will;

That I may be reasonably happy in this life and
supremely happy with Him forever in the next.
Amen.

— REINHOLD NIEBUHR

ACKNOWLEDGEMENTS

"Success has a thousand fathers, failure is an orphan."
— *ANONYMOUS*

. . . .

To all who have contributed to the stories, provided inspiration, shared their Hinge, and made this book complete.

To the entire Leavener community.

To my book designer: Teri Capron of Fresh Design. What an amazing person and business.

Phil Richards at *The Indianapolis Star*.

Teri Miller of Portraiture Studios: a truly artistic experience.

Rob Ellinger of Ellinger Riggs Insurance.

John Spafford of National Tenant Network.

Karl Schubert – Beyond the Links

Dave Williams & Dr. Cindra Kamphoff of The Center for Sport and Performance.

Corey Smallwood owner of Go Performance & Fitness in Clarksburg, MD.

The Curators & Supporters: Rusty Kennedy, Patti Lewis, Joe Lorenzano, Andrew Lowe, Evan Nance, Mary Jo Petrelli, Troy Price, Devin Rose, Jason Richmond, Keith Tyner & Bob Treash.

The Interviews: Ken Dilger, Dick Dullaghan, Ben Hesen, Dr. Mike Gradeless, Jenny Moshak, Denise Praul, Steve Shaw, Joe Skovron, Mark Stockwell.

The reviewers and editors: Lauren-Bishop Weidner, Adrienne Langelier LPC, Sandy Ward Bell, Andrew Black, Nik Cross, Will Drumright, Devin Rose, Madison Shorts, Dave Sicklesteel, Joe Stonecypher, Mary & Mitch Towe.

My family: Nicole, what an amazing woman and mother. You've seen the struggle and the triumphs—Thanks to Betty Bell for the *Reader's Digest*. My children: Ryan and Porter, love you all so much.

REFERENCES

"There are two paths you can go by."
— *LED ZEPPELIN*

. . . .

1. Wooden, J. (1997). *Wooden: A lifetime of observations and reflections on and off the court.* Chicago, IL : Contemporary Books.

2. Aerosmith & Davis, S. (1997). *Walk this way: The autobiography of Aerosmith.* New York, NY: HarperCollins.

3. Finder, C. (2000, December 26). Immaculate reception was their baby. *Pittsburgh Post-Gazette.*

4. Reiss, M. (2008, June 1). 'The Catch' won't haunt Harrison. *The Boston Globe.*

5. MJD (2012, Feb 5). The Wes Welker drop probably cost the Patriots the Super bowl. *Yahoo-Sports.*

6. Calliat, K. & Stiefel, S. (2012). Making Rumours: The Inside Story of the Classic Fleetwood Mac Album. *Wiley.*

7. Sinek, S. (2011). *Start with why: How great leaders inspire everyone to take action.* New York, NY: Portfolio/Penguin.

8. McKagan, D. (2012). *It's so easy: and other lies.* New York, NY: Touchstone.

9. Perez, D. (2011, February 10). Remembering Jerry Sloan: The NBA's last one-trick pony. *The Huffington Post.*

10. Hilton, L. (n.d.). Jansen persevered despite Olympic disappointments. *ESPN Classics.*

11. Garrity, J. (1991, August 19). Over drive: Belting mammoth tee shots, John Daly won the PGA with an awesome display of power golf. *Sports Illustrated.*

12. PEP. (2007, December 18). [Web log message] 20 Years of Bad Boys: Writer's strike helped launch Cops.

13. Graham, B. A. (2010, March 17). Two seconds that shaped a lifetime. *Sports Illustrated.*

14. Bierman, J., Smith, C. (2003) *Alamein: War Without Hate.* Penguin Books.

15. Tarbox, J. M. (1985, March 29). The day Buddy Holly died: Bobby Vee remembers. *Chicago Tribune.*

16. Dom Dimaggio. (n.d.). In Wikipedia.

17. Suzanne Bange. (2012, September 8). [youtube video] Jeffrey Maier.

18. Petty, T. (2007). *Running down a dream. Tom Petty and The Heartbreakers.* Chronicle Books.

19. Warner, C. (2013). *And then they won gold: Stepping stones to swimming excellence.* Arete aquatic services.

20. Brown, C. (2013). Sporting News conversation with Joe Namath: 'The guarantee was basically just an attitude'. *Sporting News NFL.*

21. Rosenthal, R.; Jacobson, L. (1968). *Pygmalion in the classroom.* New York: Holt, Rinehart & Winston.

22. (2007, November 1). How to cheat without cheating: Athletes and the placebo effect. *The Economist.*

23. WRF Staff. (2009). *The power of mind and the promise of placebo.*

24. (2013, May). Rocky road to success, Dr Roger Bannister: Belief beyond limits. *Be The Best You.*

25. Mills, B. (1974). 20 seconds of pain. *Journal of American Indian Education,* 13, 3.

26. Vickers, J.N. and Adolphe, R. (1997) Gaze behaviour while tracking an object and aiming at a far target. *International Journal of Sports Vision* 44, 18-27. Ken

27. Overman, S. J. (1999). "'Winning isn't Everything. It's the Only Thing': The Origin, Attributions and Influence of a Famous Football Quote," *Football Studies,* 2, 2.

28. Dilger (personal interview).

29. Brown, B. (2012). *Daring greatly: How the courage to be vulnerable transforms the way we live, love, parent, and lead.* New York, NY: Gotham Books.

30. Lee, P. (2003 November 19). Classic catches up with Lorenzo Charles. *ESPN Classic.*

31. Loder, W. (2006 October 16). When a child dies. The Compassionate Friends, Inc.

32. Finerman, W., Starkey, S., Tisch, S., Newirth, C. (Producer), & Zemeckis, R. (Director). (1994). *Forrest Gump* [Motion picture]. United States: Paramount Pictures.

33. Cargile, J. (1992). *Pascal's Wager, in Contemporary Perspectives on Religious Epistemology,* (eds.) R. Douglas Geivett and Brendan Sweetman, Oxford University Press.

34. Manoyan, D. (2012, July 7). A 1998 victory in the U.S. that still resonates in South Korea. *The New York Times.*

35. Mattson, J. E. (2005). *Been there, done that. Reflections on Nursing LEADERSHIP,* 10-36.

36. Coomarasamy, J. (2012, June 22). London 2012: Village at the heart of Kenya's running dominance. *BBC.*

37. Barry Mcguigan explains Cuban boxing success. (2013, April 18). *BBC.*

38. Cassidy, R. (2000). *History of Cuban boxing part 2: Olympic champions, defecting stars and a nation in decline.*

39. Ruby Tuesday (n.d.) in Wikipedia

40. Burger, Timothy (2002). Prez taps maverick for surgeon general. *Daily News.*

41. Jenny Moshak (Personal Interview).

42. Litsky, F. (1992, June 28). Olympics: O'Brien fails to make Olympic decathlon team. *The New York Times*

43. Gustafson, M. (2012, June 29). *Replacing third place tears.*

44. Winkler, I. (Producer), & Scorsese, M. (Director). (1990). *Goodfellas* [Motion picture]. United States: Warner Bros.

45. Sweetenham, B. (2012). *The Making of Champions* [PDF].

46. Weintraub, J. (Producer), & Avildsen, J.G. (Director). (1984). *The Karate Kid* [Motion picture]. United States: Columbia Picture.

47. *Flashback:* (2012, January 13). *When Sampras wept.*

48. NBC Sports. (2010, August 4). *In which the Out of Bounds intern interviews Jerry Rice.*

49. Hill-Patterson, T. (1997). "Whitey" inducted into hall of fame. *Times Daily.*

50. ArkansasSports360.com Staff. (2012, August 3). Pro football Hall of Fame never a dream for Roaf, but now reality. *Arkansas Business.*

51. Associated Press (1999, July 25). Robin Yount thanks friends. *A.P. News Archive.*

52. Academy of Achievement (1991, June 28). Herschel Walker interview: Gridiron greatness.

53. NLL.com. (2012, July 30). Steve Dietrich voted into the NLL Hall of Fame.

54. Kekis, J. (2012, July 12). Pro baseball: Larkin took unlikely road to Hall of Fame. Go *San Angelo Standard Times*

55. Benjamin, A. (2012, August 02). Curtis Martin heads to the Hall of Fame. *The Boston Globe.*

56. Demmons, D. (2012, July 06). Four selected for induction into International Motorsport Hall of Fame. *The Birmingham News.*

57. Fernandez, B. (2012, June 06). *Thomas Hearns: a hall of fame evolution.*

58. Gundersen, E. (2012, November 11). They're still rolling at 50: The stones start it up again rehearsals uncovered rarities. *USA Today.*

59. Associated Press. (2012, July 14). Hall induction completes Capriati's turbulent journey. *The New York Times.*

60. Dulac, G. (2012, July 30). Dermontti Dawson pulls in highest honor with pro football Hall of Fame induction. *Pittsburgh Post-Gazette.*

61. Leonard, P., & Leonard, P. (2012, June 26). Adam Oates named Caps' next coach, voted into Hall of Fame along with Pavel Bure, Joe Sakic, and Mats Sundin. *NY Daily News*

62. Associated Press (2008, April 28). Ewing, Hakeem, Vitale headline 2008 Naismith Hall of Fame class. *ESPN.*

63. Wade Boggs (n.d.). In Brainyquote.com

64. Irish, O. (2003, May 31). Do you remember when Ed Moses was almost invincible. *The Observer.*

65. Steve Shaw (personal interview)

66. Rushin, S. (2012, October 02). Ref Ed Hochuli with an inside look at what he does on a typical play. *Sports Illustrated.*

67. Baker, L. (2006). What if Guy Kawasaki was the CEO of Yahoo?. *Search Engine Journal.*

68. Hardy, L. (1990). A catastrophe model of anxiety and performance. In J. G. Jones & L. Hardy (Eds.) *Stress and performance in sport.* Chichester, UK: Wiley.

69. Don Larsen. (n.d.). In Wikipedia.

70. Professional Football Hall of Fame. (2013). Raymond Berry - Hall of Fame .

71. Rodger Federer's early career. (n.d.). In Wikipedia.

72. Kotb, H. (2009, May 31). *Dateline: On tour with Taylor Swift.*

73. Morgan, G. (2012, July 06). Wimbledon 2012: Andre Agassi recalls how it felt to win his first Grand Slam title on centre court in 1992. *The Telegraph.*

74. Jeffrey R. Immelt. (n.d.) In Wikipedia

75. Jim Marshall (American football) (n.d.) In Wikipedia.

76. Dodds, T. (1988 September 24). The Seoul Games / Day 9 : Biondi, the Underdog, Ends Up Top Dog Again. *Los Angeles Times.*

77. Feinstein, J. (2007). *Last Dance: Behind the Scenes at the Final Four.* Back Bay Books.

78. Linder, D. (2004). William Jennings Bryan (1860-1925).

79. Miller, S. (1997, June 23). Mr. invincible: Country's Trace Adkins survived a bullet, a bus, and a bulldozer. *People, 47(24).*

80. Jhung, L. (2011, December 12). Danielle Balengee: Five Years Later. *Runner's World.*

81. Verducci, T. (1993, September 13). A special delivery: That was no ordinary
no-hitter Yankee Jim Abbott threw against the Indians. *Sports Illustrated.*

82. Lady Gaga. (n.d.) In Wikipedia.

83. Lengel, Edward (2005). *General George Washington.* New York: Random House Trade Paperbacks

84. Terrell, K. (2012, October 03). Johnny Unitas, a record setting quarterback who didn't care about records. *The Time-Picayune.*

85. Feilen, G. (2009, September 17). *Think and grow rich or use your noodle and get the kaboodle.*

86. History.com. (2013). May 6, 1954: Roger Bannister breaks four-minutes mile.

87. Solomon, J. (2011, April 30). Texans' first-round pick Watt driven to succeed. *Houston Chronicle.*

88. 16 days of glory - John Moffet and Rowdy Gaines - part 2. (2008, April 26). [youtube video].

89. Mark Stockwell (personal interview).

90. Seligman, M. E. P. (2006). *Learned optimism: How to change your mind and your life.* New York, NY: Pocket Books.

91. Hershiser, O., & Wolgemuth, R. (2001). *Between the Lines: Nine principles to live by.* Warner Faith.

92. Haney, H. (2013). *The Big Miss.* Three Rivers Press.

93. Morton, B. (2005, September 25). Kennedy-Nixon Debate changed politics for good. Cnn.com.

94. *Reader's Digest* (1992). Joe Theisman's Two Rings

95. Fields , B. (2002, January 11). The detour of a phenom. *Golf World,* 55(24), 34.

96. Andrade, P. (2003). *The Mistake of All Mistakes.* Militaryhistoryonline.com

97. Seanor, D. (2009, January 25). The curious case of David Gossett. *Golf Examiner.*

98. Cote, J., Macdonald, D. J., Baker, J., & Abernethy, B. (2006). When "where" is more important than "when": Birthplace and birthdate effects on the achievement of sporting expertise. *Journal of sports sciences,* 24(10), 1065-1073

99. Toss to Moss: Marshall University's Randy Moss makes a run at '97 Heisman. (1997). *Huntington Quarterly.* Issue 29.

100. English, J. (2011, October 25). What Bill Buckner said 19 days before game 6 of the '86 World Series.

101. Wegner, D. M., Schneider, D. J., Carter III, S. R., & White, T. L. (1987). Paradoxical effects of thought suppression. *Journal of Personality and Social Psychology,* 53(1), 5-13.

102. Hayes, A. (2012, July 15). Uncovered: Why the man who created Victoria's Secret jumped off the Golden Gate bridge. *Elite Daily.*

103. Glier, R. (2005, July 07). Is Tennessee football out of bounds? *USA Today.*

104. Swyer, A., & Golin, L. (writers) Eriq La Salle (director) (1996). *Rebound: The Legend of Earl 'The Goat' Manigault* [motion picture]: United States: HBO.

105. Coleman, C. V. (2012, April 11). Lost 1: Ten years removed from comparisons to fellow VA native Allen Iverson, an incarcerated Jonathan Hargett reflects on what went wrong. Slam, (158).

106. Greenberg, J. (1990, January, 8). Daddy Dearest. *Sports Illustrated,* 72, 1.

107. Ian Jenkins-www.bigefoundation.

108. Reed, V. (2005, January, 25). *In Memory: Justin Cross, 1981-2005.* Ball State Athletics.

109. Dufresne, C. (1993, March 21). Street's Death Left An Entire State In Mourning. *Los Angeles Times.*

110. John Bissmeyer-Dadsdayindiana.com/history

111. Fran Crippen- Elevation Foundation. Francrippen.org

112. Greg Oden- Travis Smith Memorial Golf Classic hosted by Greg Oden.

. . . .

REFERENCES

Made in the USA
Middletown, DE
25 March 2016